RESET *the* HEART

Unlearning Violence, Relearning Hope

Mai-Anh Le Tran

Abingdon Press
Nashville

RESET THE HEART:
UNLEARNING VIOLENCE, RELEARNING HOPE

This book is printed on acid-free paper.

Library of Congress Cataloging-in-Publication Data has been requested.

ISBN: 978-1-5018-3246-8

Content in chapters 4–6 can be found in Mai-Anh Le Tran, "Communicability, Redeemability, Educability," in *Educating for Redemptive Community: Essays in Honor of Jack Seymour and Margaret Ann Crain*, ed. Denise Janssen (Eugene: Wipf and Stock, 2015), 95-110. Used by permission.

This book is derived, in part, from an article published in *Religious Education* on August 14, 2015, available online: http://wwww.tandfonline.com/10.1080/00344087.2015.1063960 Reprinted by permission of the Religious Education Association, (http://www.religiouseducation.net).

The list on page 53 is from Charles R. Foster, *From Generation to Generation: The Adaptive Challenge of Mainline Protestant Education in Forming Faith.* Copyright © 2012. Used by permission of Wipf and Stock Publishers. www.wipfandstock.com.

The list on page 51 is from Charles R. Foster, *Educating Congregations: The Future of Christian Education.* Copyright © 1994 by Abingdon Press. Used by permission. All rights reserved.

17 18 19 20 21 22 23 24 25 26—10 9 8 7 6 5 4 3 2 1

MANUFACTURED IN THE UNITED STATES OF AMERICA

To Amanda Phuong-Anh,
upon you we have set our hearts

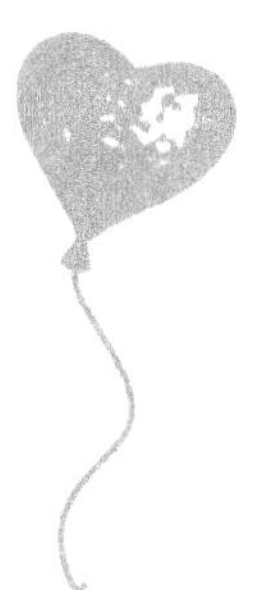

Contents

vii Acknowledgments

1 Chapter 1
The Problem of Faith in a Violent World

21 Chapter 2
*Dis*Imagination Land

47 Chapter 3
The Violence of Religious Educational Practice

77 Chapter 4
Practicing Communicability

105 Chapter 5
Practicing Redeemability

129 Chapter 6
Practicing Educability

155 Conclusion
"World Turned Upside Down"

165 Appendix

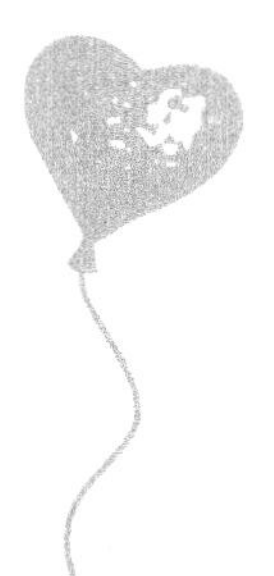

Acknowledgments

When you eat a piece of fruit, remember who planted the tree. Thus said wise Vietnamese elders. I, "chewing a piece of sugarcane" (Rumi), am grateful for the many planters of trees who made every morsel of this fruit a precious bite.

For the ways they demonstrate how scholarship should matter to the way we live, I give thanks for the students, the fourteen alums who contributed to this project, the faculty, and the leadership of Eden Theological Seminary. For the time they took to motivate, challenge, exhort, I owe special gratitude to Margaret Ann Crain, Jack Seymour, Chuck Foster, Evelyn Parker, Dori Baker, Marion Grau. For the inspirational engagement and support that made possible the 2014 conference on "Religion, Education, and the (Un)Making of Violence"—the research playground for this book—I am grateful to colleagues and board members of the Religious Education Association. For the paradigmatic question, "So are you going to do something?" and her even-keeled friendship, I thank Martha Robertson. For the number of times she corrected my writing in pencil and told me what she truly thinks of my work, I take sanctuary in the benedictions of Marilyn Stavenger. For her cheerleading, embracing, forgiving, and believing, which make me blush, I owe Andrea Bieler serious royalty. For marvelous stewardship of others' words and thoughts, I sing the praises of Ulrike Guthrie and the editorial team of Abingdon. For his diligence and inquisitiveness, I thank my task-manager Jacob. For the way he listened cautiously and knew what to draw out of me, there would be no this or that without David Teel.

And my greatest gifts: HAT, for being an accompanying gossip about theological varia; TAT, for humoring what I do for a living; my personal chef and reluctant gardener, Mom and Dad—their faith, love, hope, and courage allow me to live, move, and have being.

Acknowledgments

Chapter 1

The Problem of Faith in a Violent World

Summer Reveries[1]

"So are you going to do something?"

It was August 13, 2014, and I had just gotten back to St. Louis from New York City, and there I stood in a hair salon catching up with Martha, a colleague and friend, for a few minutes between her appointment and mine. I had no idea what her question meant.

"You know, there's talk of activities being organized around what happened over the weekend. Are you going to participate?" my friend continued with patience, as if she knew too well what it takes to recalibrate one's frame of mind after sabbatical exploits.

"You know, the shooting in Ferguson . . . ," Martha helped out.

It was breaking news, and I had not yet caught on to the names "Michael Brown" and "Darren Wilson." Martha clued me in: a White police officer fatally shot an unarmed Black teenager in a suburb less than fifteen miles north of where I live and teach.[2] The fact that I remained

1. This opening account and its rhetorical style mimic the techniques of what Heather Walton describes as "performance autoethnography," in which experience is shared as "a staged act, an intervention, a public and political display." A few interwoven analytic segments are taken from previous writing, adapted for this practical theological conversation. See Heather Walton, *Writing Methods in Theological Reflection* (London: SCM Press, 2014), 7.

2. I capitalize *Black* and *White* to signal the social constructed nature of racialized identity markers. As indicators of racial constructions, they are fluid, situational, dynamically negotiated, and contested rather than fixed qualifiers of essentialized difference.

oblivious to the news is egregious only in hindsight. After all, doesn't our social imaginary consider violent shootings involving Black youth "normal," especially for an urban metropolis like St. Louis?

Three days later, I found myself on the sidewalk of Canfield Drive, staring at a makeshift roadside memorial in the middle of the street, at the spot where a teenager's body was left lifeless and exposed for over four hours before grief-stricken, bewildered, indifferent, vulturous eyes. People were just beginning to gather for what was to be the first vigil for the fatal shooting by local law enforcement of yet another African American youth—but something was different in the air that day. Vigil keepers positioned themselves quietly. A woman evangelist with a bullhorn was proclaiming muffled words about salvation. It began to rain. Someone nearby muttered, "Rain cleanses . . ."

August 9 means different things to different people—and perhaps nothing at all to some—but it disrupted my world. I was in New York City when Eric Garner died under the chokehold of a police officer, and I had just left the San Francisco Bay Area when Oscar Grant was shot by a BART officer who mistook his own gun for a Taser. So why does the body of Michael Brown lifeless on the ground disrupt and disturb me so? Why did the moment at which I nervously sat on the public "mourning bench"[3] become for me the ominous zero-hundred-hours that marked both an ending and a beginning of something—of what I knew not at that moment?

For one, it disrupted my professional world because as soon as news broke out, members of the seminary community at which I teach as well as religious professionals and faith groups in all of greater St. Louis knew that we were going to have to snap to attention and spring into action. As facts remained muddied with stories and counter-testimonies, feet took to the streets; vigils and forums were improvised everywhere; teach-ins, preach-ins, and eat-ins were organized by local leaders, in concert with experts and partners from all over the country. In the following months, what seemed to be dramaturgical performances of religious ritual (from ecumenical Christian worship to interfaith prayer services), faith-based action, and intentional consciousness-raising efforts gave evidence of a social

3. Nicholas Wolterstorff, *Lament for a Son* (Grand Rapids: W. B. Eerdmans, 1987), 34.

collective being spiritually reconfigured by tragedy.[4] The activities tested the capacity of faith communities to engage in disciplined improvisation: after all, we are in the business of "making disciples for the transformation of the world"[5]—can we walk the faith talk at such a violent time as this?

As the context-specific actions of Ferguson merged with the larger #BlackLivesMatter protest movement,[6] local lay and clergy leaders learned anew what it takes to "put some feet to their prayers." However, as improvisational efforts continued to rally and organize churches toward the enduring work of confronting the insidious violence of systemic social injustices in their own backyard, these leaders ran head-on into a familiar yet perplexing wall: *the incapacity and unwillingness of their faith communities to respond with some form of faith-driven action.* In many cases, the resistance was (and still is) fierce, eerily reminiscent of the stand-offs that divided racialized religious communities and civic leadership in the 1960s civil rights era. If the church's teaching, learning, and practice of faith is purportedly transformative, then *where is that faith when it is needed most*? If "good" religious formation had been happening all along—or had it?—then why the indifference, paralysis, apathy, exasperation, and even downright resistance when a calamity occurred that could have used a faithful response? Why does it appear as if collective moral consciousness has once again been anesthetized, and the hope for which church folk love to sing and pray suddenly debilitated in the face of actual struggle? The problem is perplexing. Anemic prayers for peace seem impotent, and steady obedience to the long haul of faithful action seems dissatisfying when the very foundations of faith seems to be quaking due to human tantrums.

The killing of Michael Brown disrupted my professional world, but it also disturbed my very psyche, triggering a crisis of faith· if you will—albeit a variety suffered by those who can afford to call existential certitude into question and not have to worry about what to eat, where to live,

4. See a chronicle of these events captured through recounted first-person narratives in Leah Gunning Francis, *Ferguson & Faith: Sparking Leadership & Awakening Community* (St. Louis: Chalice Press, 2015).

5. This is the motto of The United Methodist Church.

6. The campaign began with the killing of Trayvon Martin by George Zimmerman in Florida. See http://blacklivesmatter.com.

whom to love, or whether or not we would survive the next day. Nonetheless, it was a crisis of faithful meaning-making: What does it mean to be a person of faith in a violent world? What does it even mean to "have faith" in this world that is so violent? What does it mean for vulnerable bodies—victims of systemic and systematic abuse, neglect, and indifference—to continue believing that this world exists for them, for their future, for their flourishing? What does it mean for any of us to continue about our daily business of eating, praying, and loving, when the world continues to be punctured and ruptured by violence? If *faith* is a *verb*, then how do we "do it" in such a world that we have today?

Resetting the Heart

The above questions and the larger-than-life issues they convey are vexing for me as a person of faith, an ordained minister in a church that proclaims commitment to transformative work in the world, and a scholar of religious educational praxis.[7] Unfolding world events reflect both the fertility and fragility of our everyday *chronos* time. Religions teach love of neighbor, but reality reminds us repeatedly that it is hard to know who is neighbor and who is enemy. After all, in many times and places, we are both neighbor and enemy to one another. Despite forecasts about rising secularism and post-religious, post-Christian movements in North America, we have empirical descriptions of exploding charismatic spiritualities and groundswells of new "Christendoms" in the global south.[8] The transnational flows of peoples have collapsed contexts, but have also exposed the fierce reflexes of physical and social immune systems triggered by risky human contact. Opportunities to share meals, fellowship, and prayers with new friends across the globe remind us of the early Christian communities' seemingly ideal habits (Acts 2:42). But the allergens and pathogens—biological and social—contracted during border-crossings

7. *Praxis* is the melding of theory and practice; it is the integration of reflective action and practice-based reflection. Praxis is a notable development for religious education and its use by Brazilian educational reformer Paulo Freire is an important source of inspiration.

8. Philip Jenkins, *The Next Christendom: The Coming of Global Christianity*, 3rd ed. (Oxford; New York: Oxford University Press, 2011).

also remind us of how these basic human activities of eating, praying, and loving challenge our notions of what it means to be "redemptive community."[9] Every now and then, standing in liminal, *chronos* time, we gasp for *kairos* hope, because "we can't breathe." . . . Attending to such moments, scholars-practitioners of religious education ask, What does it mean to *teach for faith* in such a time as this?

I have had several occasions to drive pass the spot—marked now by a memorial plaque—where Mike Brown's body lay for over four hours. When the world is not watching and the theatricality of news-reporting has left, the place is quiet, even serene. Yet, Canfield Drive and other blood- and rain-soaked grounds like it continue to give off "ghost flames,"[10] haunting the public conscience with grief and rage that calls for a less violent, more just world. The paradigmatic event of #Ferguson—an event that reflects the current implosive outrage against structural inequities in society and culture—raises questions for religious leadership and religious teaching and learning. For many such leaders, the demands for change from the streets are challenging our existing "curriculum" for "faith as practice." The world is demanding from people of faith—Christians in the United States, in particular—an account of how our faith is evidenced in the gritty and murderous materiality of everyday life.

Perhaps over the years, teaching and learning in Christian religious communities have obsessed too much with the *structure*, *contents*, and *infrastructures* of faith. That is to say, we dissect the constitutive elements of meaning-making that help us make sense of certain faith positions (structure); we debate about what is the correct object of our spiritual allegiance and moral-ethical bearing (content);[11] and we fret about the sustainability

9. See Denise Janssen, ed., *Educating for Redemptive Community: Essays in Honor of Jack Seymour and Margaret Ann Crain* (Eugene: Wipf and Stock, 2015).

10. Grace M. Cho, *Haunting the Korean Diaspora: Shame, Secrecy, and the Forgotten War* (Minneapolis, MN: University of Minnesota Press, 2008), 16.

11. See a critique of religious education's overzealous rapprochement of psychosocial-structural developmental theories in Romney Moseley's essay, "Education and Human Development in the Likeness of Christ," in *Theological Approaches to Christian Education*, ed. Jack L. Seymour and Donald E. Miller (Nashville: Abingdon Press, 1990).

of our resources to transmit our faith systems (infrastructure).[12] Amid these efforts, we sometimes forget that the lifelong and lifewide[13] *processes* of forging, fashioning, nurturing, and exercising our faith require relational, evolving, and even revolutionary commitment to our surrounding *contexts*. We neglect the Christian tradition's long-held reverence for *phronesis*—or, as Don Browning defines it, the "wisdom that attends to lived experience, is transformative and change-seeking and *always* interprets the lived context in the light of the values and virtues of sacred tradition."[14] It is this commitment to *practical wisdom* that keeps our teaching, learning, and practice of faith incarnational. This commitment makes us want to see how faith actually (re)orders our way of life. Theologically speaking, we are eager to "trac[e] the form God wears in this material world,"[15] and we believe that such discovery of and participation with "God in our skin"—*Immanu-El*—is what it would take to mend the broken shards of creation (*tikkun Olam*). With this primordial human desire to repair our world we muster up *faith*, to "set our hearts"[16] upon things that are at once material and ethereal, s**** and holy, momentary and eternal, this-worldly and other-worldly. It is this gritty kind of faith that helps us not to be flummoxed when confronted with the question, "Are you going to do something in response to this violence?"

Theologians and educators have persisted in articulating the enduring pursuit of both faith and understanding, in pondering whether there will be faith in the coming future, and speculating about the nature of emergent faith forms.[17] Time and again, I return to the eloquence of James W.

12. Charles F. Foster's assessment of educational infrastructures in establishment church will be the subject of discussion in chapter 3.

13. Gabriel Moran, *Living Nonviolently: Language for Resisting Violence* (Lanham, MD: Lexington Books, 2011).

14. Don S. Browning, *A Fundamental Practical Theology: Descriptive and Strategic Proposals* (Minneapolis, MN: Fortress Press, 1991), 47; cited in Heather Walton, *Writing Methods in Theological Reflection,* 176–77. Emphasis in original text.

15. Walton, *Writing Methods in Theological Reflection,* 40.

16. Sara Little's iconic book title and her treatment of "credo" will be the foundation for further development in later chapters. Sara Little, *To Set One's Heart: Belief and Teaching in the Church* (Atlanta: John Knox Press, 1983).

17. Daniel L. Migliore, *Faith Seeking Understanding: An Introduction to Christian Theology* (Grand Rapids: W. B. Eerdmans, 1991); Harvey Gallagher Cox, *The Future of Faith* (New York: HarperOne, 2009); Thomas H. Groome, *Will There Be Faith? A New Vision for Educating and Growing Disciples* (New York: HarperOne, 2011).

Fowler, who, to the chagrin of many, dared to propose structure to Mystery through the empirical sciences, but who, borrowing the theological constructs of his contemporaries, gave language to a human phenomenon that many of us could only timidly describe as "gift":

> For most of us, most of the time, faith functions so as to screen off the abyss of mystery that surrounds us. But we all at certain times call upon faith to provide nerve to stand in the presence of the abyss—naked, stripped of life supports, trusting only in the being, the mercy and the power of the Other in the darkness. Faith helps us form a dependable "life space," an ultimate environment. At a deeper level, faith undergirds us when our life space is punctured and collapses, when the felt reality of our ultimate environment proves to be less than ultimate.[18]

Faith, it seems, is this primal capacity to inhabit our world, and to imbue our muddling through it with some sense of meaning and purpose, even if provisionally. Faith is what undergirds us when we confront the vicissitudes of life—the murder of an innocent teenager by an officer of the law, for example—and allows us to grapple with the full scope of human (and planetary) suffering and hope. In Christian theological dialects, we could call this the range between *theodicy* and *ecstasy*. Faith nourishes a courage—the root word for which is *coeur*, the heart—for a *re-enchantment* and *re-sacralization* of this world. It allows us to ask a blunt question: What does it mean to reset the heart for faith—and for love and hope (1 Cor 13:13)—in the afterburn of violence, in the afterburn of whatever is this week's #Ferguson?

Theodicy and Ecstasy in the Afterburn of #Ferguson[19]

"Afterburn" became a haunting expression after a seminarian brought to me a section from an old training manual that she had kept from her

18. James W. Fowler, *Stages of Faith: The Psychology of Human Development and the Quest for Meaning* (San Francisco: Harper & Row, 1981), xii.

19. The popular Twitter hashtag format # is used here to mark how Ferguson, a city of some twenty thousand-plus residents, has become a paradigmatic world in both actual and virtual reality.

days in the police academy in the state of Colorado. The term *afterburn* appears in the section on "street survival":

> There's a psychological violence connected with gunfights that can be a dangerous enemy, as well as the physical violence. . . . Sometimes the effect makes itself felt almost immediately. . . . Most often, though, the impact is not so swift for the officer. It's likelier to set in days, weeks, even months after the shooting, through a phenomenon some therapists call "after-burn." This refers to the tendency of the human mind to dwell on unpleasant, emotion-charged events in the wake of their actual occurrence. In afterburn, you relive and react to an experience, churning over and over what you and others did and what you might or should have done different. This continual reminding and reassessing can be as vivid as the original event—and even more psychologically upsetting.[20]

Here, therapeutic advisement to members of law enforcement makes it plain that the taking of human life is empirically disturbing, unsettling, and traumatic, even for individuals involved on the "right" side of the law, the "winning" side. One wonders, what of the afterburn for the wider socio-cultural psyche in the aftermath of events like #Ferguson, in which unjust state actions and merciless social reactions continue to churn, to haunt, to re-image themselves as vivid reminders to a suffering people of the enduring problem of *theodicy*: "If God is on the side of the [oppressed]—why don't they win?"[21]

How will the teaching of faith assist people in addressing such a question?

Now, the grammar of Christian theology insists that to speak of suffering is to foreshadow hope, and I am drawn to reframing Christian hope in terms of *ecstasy*, persuaded by Philip Wexler's proposal for a "reenchantment" or "resacralization" of education.[22] In this paradigm, educators might imagine themselves as magicians who—"endowed with charisma"

20. Charles Remsberg, Ronald J. Adams, and Thomas M. McTernan, *Street Survival: Tactics for Armed Encounters* (Northbrook: Calibre Press, 1980), 283–84.

21. Walton, *Writing Methods in Theological Reflection*, 150.

22. Philip Wexler, *Holy Sparks: Social Theory, Education, and Religion* (New York: St. Martin's Press, 1996).

("that extraordinary personal power") and elevated above the realm of the ordinary in their ecstatic state—offer some sense of meaning and order to "a world disenchanted and losing magical significance."[23] What if religious educators were also to imagine themselves endowed, not so much with the extraordinary prototypical charisma to be singularly elevated from the rest, but rather with the *charism*[24] to facilitate the ecstatic reenchantment, resacralization of lives "cut dead" by society?[25]

Such questions frame the agenda for this book. The 1960s and '70s yielded prodigious theories and theologies for revolutionary social change in US contexts. And yet, on August 9, 2014, religious folks once again found lumps in their throats. As unrest ensued over that one death, a death that many other violent outbreaks around the world have joined since then, we wonder whether there will *ever* be change for good. If transformative religious teaching and learning had been happening all along, then why the indifference, paralysis, apathy, exasperation, resistance, vitriolic public discourse and micro-aggressive exchanges on social media, altogether symptoms of corroded moral conscience and debilitated hope, every time violence occurs among us in varied forms and magnitudes, in such places as Nice, Baton Rouge, Dallas, Orlando, Ansbach, Istanbul, Davao?

One answer may come in a searing indictment: that in our pluralistic yet also politicized, polarizing, and racialized world, even progressive Christian faith communities are still culturally captive and our stories/theologies and rituals/practices of the faith continue to anesthetize moral agency and debilitate courageous action for hope and change.

This book invites risky exploration of the above premise. Three paradigmatic questions guide our practical concerns:

23. Wexler, "Religion as Socio-Educational Critique: A Weberian Example," in *Critical Pedagogy: Where Are We Now?*, ed. Peter McLaren and Joe L. Kincheloe, Counterpoints: Studies in the Postmodern Theory of Education (New York: Peter Lang, 2007), 51–52.

24. Kathleen A. Cahalan, *Introducing the Practice of Ministry* (Collegeville: Liturgical Press, 2010), 31.

25. See Gregory C. Ellison, *Cut Dead but Still Alive: Caring for African American Young Men* (Nashville: Abingdon Press, 2013).

1. What does it mean to educate for faith in a world marked by violence?
2. How are Christian faith communities complicit in the teaching and learning of violence?
3. What new (or *renewed*) practices of faith and educational leadership can help us unlearn violence and relearn hope?

This exploration is driven by a hope-based conviction: that violence challenges our Christian communities to regenerate radical forms of prophetic, (pro)tested faith, and to hone those skills and instincts through public conscientization and participatory action, whose goal is insurrectional, resurrectional hope.

There lies the agenda for resetting the heart.

The first half of this book is devoted to problem-posing. In this first chapter, we wrestle with the first paradigmatic question: *What does it mean to teach for faith in a violent world?* Spun differently, what *is* faith in the afterburn of violence? In chapter 2, we examine a social constructivist analysis of violence's pedagogic roots. Focusing on specific events of racial/ethnic and religious violence in the United States and other parts of the world, I draw on the analytic frameworks of social psychology, cultural studies, postcolonial theory, and racial formation theory to suggest that violence has public pedagogic implements—instructional tools—that breed toxic social fear of and indifference to "the other."

The discussion leads to the second paradigmatic question, a challenging question for Christian faith communities: *How is the church complicit in the teaching and learning of violence?*

A plausible answer to that question is offered in chapter 3, where we recall—with some reframing—Charles Foster's critiques in his two books, *Educating Christians* and *From Generation to Generation.* As Foster did, beyond challenging the major "flaws" of the church's "catechetical cultures," this chapter suggests how a Christian faith community may in practice be a "community of violence."[26] The reframing of Foster's analyses of five major flaws are the following:

Foster	**Re-Framed**
Loss of corporate memory	Erasure of historical memory
Irrelevant biblical teaching	The Bible as "weapon of mass destruction"
Subversion of educational goals	Pedagogic habitus of disimagination
Cultural captivity	The church as fractured sanctuary
Collapse of educational strategies	Banking educational curricula

What follows this problem-posing is an attempt to map consciousness-raising for appropriate action. The second half of the book answers the third paradigmatic question: *What (re)new(ed) practices of faith yield potential for the unlearning and unmaking of violence?* To do so, we break down what it means to imagine a faith that is *tested* and *testing*, *protested* and *protesting* in the thick of contemporary social dis-ease, reflected in such public outcries as #OccupyReligion, #ShutItDown, #ICan'tBreathe. It is a faith that draws upon the reservoirs of the biblical (prophetic), theological (postcolonial, intercultural), and historical (liberationist) traditions, but is recalibrated for the intersectional, interstitial social pain of our time. "(Pro) Tested faith" calls upon several deliberate pedagogic strategies that address the fatal flaws of religious formation, with the aim of re-conscientizing communities of faith for restorative, reconciling, renewing, reforming action in the world.

Chapters 4–6 present a development of three themes that anchor an agenda for critical teaching toward resurrectional, insurrectional hope: *communicability*, *redeemability*, and *educability*. The themes are further illustrated by examples of strategies observed by local Christian faith leaders who are serving in specific faith communities in the greater St. Louis area

26. Hannah Arendt, *On Violence* (New York: Harcourt, 1970), 67.

and beyond. The witnesses of these ministers—ordained and lay—represent a treasure trove of practical wisdom concerning the human capacity to respond to insidious violence through communicable hope, redeemable faith, and educable hope. Throughout this discovery, we hold up as signposts stories of "ghost flames"—those bodies stripped of vitality due to social deaths—to awaken imagination and to portend the catastrophic consequences of religious inaction.

To illustrate the challenges and possibilities of the above agenda, I return to scenes from Ferguson, October 13, 2014.

Lessons from the Streets

As soon as news broke across the country about the shooting death of Michael Brown on August 9, clergy, faith leaders, and religious organizations in metropolitan St. Louis intuitively knew that they had to spring into action. As facts remained muddied with stories and counter-stories, feet took to the streets under the rallying cry *#PrayingWithOurFeet*. That first solemn vigil on August 16 kicked off a whirlwind of actions, eventually escalating into a national and global movement of anguished, tenacious, combustive protests.

Before the police shooting of a Black teenager on one ordinary midday metamorphosed into a sensational "Ferguson event" that shook up a nation, the local activists and clergy leaders who showed up to that first vigil continued to show up: at rallies, marches, forums, town halls, teach-ins, preach-ins, eat-ins, meetings with government officials, meetings with enraged citizens. Before a movement took shape, before commercial banners marketing solidarity were lifted against the St. Louis skyline, before eloquent open letters by public figures made front pages, before gubernatorial leadership appointed yet another commission[27] to look into the historical arc of structural disparities and racialized animus, these local activists and religious leaders "prayed with their feet" and exercised disciplined

27. "The Ferguson Commission is an empowered, independent and diverse group that will study the underlying social and economic conditions underscored by the unrest in the wake of the death of Michael Brown." It is composed of sixteen St. Louis-area residents of diverse makeup and professional backgrounds, all appointed by Missouri's Governor Jay Nixon. "Stl Positive Change: Official Site of the Ferguson Commission," http://stlpositivechange.org/.

improvisation. The public will always expect messianic stars to emerge out of a movement, but even the media had to acknowledge that besides the few "grass-tops" who make the billboards, at the grassroots level this cooperative is *leader-full. The Huffington Post* named them collectively as "people of the year" at the close of 2014.[28]

As the movement continues to unfold, I refrain from singling out individual leaders. However, moments, incidents, and events do stand out. One in particular was a Moral Monday held on October 13, 2014, the culminating event for a Weekend of Resistance in a series of Ferguson October actions.[29] On that day, I saw bodies employed as public pedagogies—mediums and instruments of instruction for a wide-eyed public.

Bodily Testimonies

The Weekend of Resistance was organized from multiple bases across St. Louis. With so many moving parts and tag-team leadership, anxious participants were receiving information from every direction and through all sorts of mediums—texts, e-mails, phone calls, word of mouth. Grand-scale marches and public forums were scheduled for Friday through Sunday, but Monday was going to be a Moral Monday, modeled after the movement of demonstrations and civil disobedience led by religious leadership of North Carolina in 2013, in protest against the state's legislative actions.[30] For Ferguson's Moral Monday, faith leaders across the religious spectrum—some who for theological reasons ordinarily would not have thought to stand beside their newly allied colleagues—took to the streets

28. HuffPost Religion Editors, "Huffpost Religion's People of the Year Are the Religious Leaders of Ferguson," *The Huffington Post,* December 29, 2014, http://m.huffpost.com/us/entry/6373064.

29. Sara Sidner, "Activist Cornel West among 49 People Arrested at Ferguson Protests," *CNN,* October 13, 2014, www.cnn.com/2014/10/13/us/ferguson-protests/; "More Than 50 Arrested at Ferguson Police Station on 'Moral Monday,' Other Events Elsewhere," *ST. Louis Post-Dispatch,* October 13, 2014, www.stltoday.com/news/local/crime-and-courts/more-than-arrested-at-ferguson-police-station-on-moral-monday/article_c1752132-9731-542e-8525-1885fae7fd10.html.

30. Yonat Shimron, "NAACP's William Barber Emerges as Leader of Moral Monday Protests," *Religion News Service,* June 24, 2013, www.religionnews.com/2013/06/24/naacps-william-barber-emerges-as-leader-of-moral-monday-protests/.

of Ferguson to express public solidarity with the local activism of the entire weekend. The plan was to engage in a peaceful march from a local United Methodist church to the Ferguson Police Department, where the group of several hundred laypeople and clergy would enact what they had intended to be a public liturgy of *remembrance*, *lament*, and *repentance*. A number of clergy had indicated their willingness to risk arrest. No one knew how things would unfold.[31]

The church was packed that morning. The organizers led an orientation. Clergy prayed. All sang. Peacekeepers and de-escalators huddled to review sketches of marching routes and formations, each etching onto their arms the phone number for bail support.

After some hours of waiting, it began. With camera crews awaiting to capture "breaking news," the doors of that church were flung open, and a wall of arms-locked bodies, clad in religious garb, proceeded steadily and rhythmically into the street. With echoing defiance, they bellowed the words to that familiar spiritual: *"Ain't gonna let nobody turn me'round . . . turn me'round . . . turn me'round . . ."* No camera, no marshal, no police, not even the rain was going to stop them. One block after another they walked, until finally they reached the Ferguson Police Department. A line of police officers received them. The public liturgy formally began—*leitourgia*, after all, is the "public work of the people."[32]

As the rain hardened, voices of students, professors, clergy, and laity bellowed,

> We are here to claim this public space as sacred space.
> we are here to declare sacred the actions already taken in Michael Brown's name
> we are here to consecrate the words already declared for Michael Brown, whose blood is still crying out in the streets
> we are here to call together a holy community, standing in solidarity with youth who have been protesting in the streets for 60+ days

31. See F. Willis Johnson, *Holding Up Your Corner: Talking about Race in Your Community* (Nashville: Abingdon Press, 2017).

32. Thomas H. Groome, *Will There Be Faith?*, 166.

> We are here to retell stories we have learned about the life of Michael Brown.
> Michael Brown is more than the name of a movement for racial equality and justice.[33]

After the entire litany was read, a chalk outline was drawn on the rain-soaked pavement. A line of clergy leaders stepped up close to face each police officer standing at the receiving line. They began to address the officers, each in their own manner—some with vehemence, others softly—all pleading for contrition and repentance. A few officers exchanged quiet words with their confessors; most maintained their resolve not to engage.[34]

It was pouring by then. The clergy continued talking and praying. The crowd closed in with anxious curiosity. Peacekeepers and de-escalators gripped one another's hands to form a human fence between the clergy up front who were risking arrest and the rest of the crowd behind them. Bodies grew restless and pushed closer. Organizers kept pleading and instructing various sections to take steps back, but energetic individuals broke through the buffer zone in disregard. However, each time the peacekeepers fumbled to close the gaps, individuals from the crowd would step up and grab their hands. The buffer zone restabilized each time. The day's action was leader-full.

The news media have their formulaic headlines for such events, like, "[*x*] number of people, led by [*so and so*—insert high-profile names], were arrested in a demonstration of [*y* number of monolithic people] in some disorderly confrontation with *z* number of uniform law enforcement." However, as we know, stories from muddy and bloody grounds ring multivalent notes—contradictory, paradoxical, ironic, even self-incriminating. For four hours and thirty minutes—symbolic of the length of time Michael Brown's body lay on the ground on Canfield Drive—plus many more hours before and after, the protesters in Ferguson on that Moral Monday endured body-numbing torrential rain to enact multifaith

33. The litany was coauthored by two students of Eden Theological Seminary. Used by permission.

34. See a description of this event in Jim Wallis, *America's Original Sin: Racism, White Privilege, and the Bridge to a New America* (Grand Rapids: Brazos Press, 2016).

leitourgia. They were certainly not of one mind about causes and effects, but each was impelled to use their body as public witness—public work—against what they believed to be unjust application of law. There lies the potency of *bodies as testimony*—bodies practicing *marturia*, the bearing of public witness, even at risky costs.[35] A body bleeding on the ground . . . a body, arms locked with another's . . . a body drenched to shivers . . . a body shielded uneasily behind riot gear . . . a body twisted in sorrow . . . a body stiffened by anger . . . a body elongated by the hand of a stranger . . . each one teaching us lessons about the practice of lived faith when communities are fractured by contact. As religious educators have also described, these bodies became implements of sacramental teaching—bodies that "mediated the Holy" for a wide-eyed public, bodies caught up in a state of *mimetic ecstasy* with the hope that justice would be timely delivered.

Mimetic Ecstasy

In her 2002 presidential address to the Religious Education Association, Anne Streaty Wimberly dared scholars of religious education to envision their vocation as one of "leadership with hope."[36] Drawing on the work of Mary Elizabeth Mullino Moore, Wimberly conceptualizes Christian religious leadership as sacramental, in that it is the work of "mediating the Holy" through specific educative practices: facilitating the remembrance of God's demand for justice and shalom; expressing such theo-ethical, theo-political imperatives through both word and deed; raising people's critical consciousness to the gaps between vision and reality; and creating opportunities for people to re-emplot—to re-story—their lives according to God's economies of justice.[37]

35. For religious education, we consider *bodies as public pedagogies*—bodies as means of explicit and implicit public instruction. Groome, *Will There Be Faith?*, 165.

36. Anne Streaty Wimberly, "Daring to Lead with Hope," *Religious Education* 98, no. 3 (2003).

37. Ibid., 283–84. See Mary Elizabeth Moore, *Teaching as a Sacramental Act* (Cleveland, OH: Pilgrim Press, 2004). Moore's hermeneutics for sacramental teaching include expecting the unexpected; remembering the disremembered; seeking reversals; giving thanks; nourishing life; reconstructing community and repairing the world.

By following Wimberly's (and Moore's) constructions, we can detect two instructive aspects of the testifying bodies of the Ferguson protestors on that Moral Monday. First, their bodies became formidable *mnemonic devices* for a public in need of serious schooling—about historic injuries suffered by enslaved peoples, about insidious systemic disparities that privilege some and diminish the livelihood of others, about complex societal technologies that manage fear and security extending far beyond what we flatly call "police brutality." Bodies on the ground, on the streets, on their knees, on their feet "urge, prod, dare, and encourage" people not to forget.[38]

Second, protesting bodies presented a *mimetic opportunity* for those watching.[39] When the leader-full teaching bodies of Ferguson marched out into the streets, they became mnemonic devices that urged mimetic reenactment elsewhere in greater St. Louis, the country, and the global community. Perhaps we can call it *mimetic ecstasy*—a mimesis, a fractal mirroring[40] of ecstatic reenchantment, as bodies spilled into the streets to re-sacralize defiled grounds and re-consecrate degraded spirits.

Like mystical incantations, the words of the public litany on that Moral Monday reverberated in the rain:

> We are here because we recognize that people and institutions have failed to honor the sacredness of all human life . . .
> We are here because the Ferguson Police Department responded with violence, rather than compassion . . .
> We are here because yards are for barbeques and not for tear gas . . .

38. Wimberly writes, "I want to emphasize the connection of education to leadership by highlighting education as 'leading out' with particular emphasis on modeling or going out ahead to show the way and of *urging, prodding, daring,* and *encouraging* others to accept as central to their own plot-making the care of the earth's people and the earth." Italics added. Wimberly, "Daring to Lead with Hope," 287.

39. Ibid., 281. Her use of *mimesis* follows Paul Riceour's terminology and construct. See Paul Ricœur, *Time and Narrative*, 3 vols. (Chicago: University of Chicago Press, 1984).

40. One could ask, how is ecstasy and enchantment mimicable? I draw on the analogy of fractals to entertain the notion that no pattern of repetition is ever the same, yet each act encourages another. Additionally, one could ask about the shadow dimensions to protest in the streets, such as ill-planned actions that yield less-than-instructive effects. I acknowledge such legitimate line of inquiry, and concede that it is beyond the scope of this book.

We are here because when protestors are held on bail set at thousands of dollars, youth are being priced out of their right to speak . . .
We are here because black youth find more community on the streets than in our churches . . .
We are here because the media tells a story where black folks are responsible for their own oppression . . .
We are here because rich kids get taught, poor kids get tested, and Michael Brown never got to go to college . . .
We are here because trash is collected with more dignity than was given to the body of Michael Brown . . .
We are here because the whole damn system is guilty as hell.

Black Lives Matter. All Lives Matter[41]
We who believe in freedom cannot rest until it comes. Until the killing of black men, black mothers' sons, is as important as the killing of white men, white mothers' sons, we cannot rest.
We are called by the lives of Michael Brown, Kajieme Powell, VonDerrit Myers, and all lives cut short by police brutality to create a world where all lives matter.
We are challenged by the protestors who declare that all lives matter, day and night, to believe that our actions matter.
Today, our actions proclaim that our lives are sacred, our resistance is holy, and in the name of Michael Brown, Kajieme Powell, VonDerrit Myers, and all lives cut short by police brutality, this street is our sacred, holy space.
We are challenged by the protesters who have courageously faced police every night, claiming this space by daring to imagine a world where blackness is not a weapon or a crime.

Because of this, we say: Whose street?
Our street!
Whose street?
Our street![42]

---

41. The seminarians who composed this portion of the litany did eventually come to learn about the contentious politics that pitted the ideological commitments behind "Black Lives Matter" against those driving the "All Lives Matter" rhetoric. I am inclined to think that the juxtaposition of these two declarations is an effective reframing of oppositional discourse.

42. All of this is part of the long litany cited earlier, coauthored by the students of Eden

A Heart Set for Faith

The young leaders of the Ferguson and Black Lives Matter movement, known as Millennial Activists, made it clear that they had no use for the vapid religious gestures of establishment religion.[43] Instead, they were more compelled by how religious folk learned how to "trace the forms God wears" in the streets. When choruses of protest insisted, "This is what theology looks like!" a religious educator recognizes that the testimony is not one of doctrinal coherence or unity. The crowd did not mean to say, "This is our theology, this is our belief," for we would be hard pressed to find two people of the same faith who would have been able to give the same lucid theological rationale for why their bodies were in the streets that day. "This is what theology looks like *in practice*," they intuited. As religious educator Karen Tye tells her students about the art of quilting, "If you don't know what to think (about what to make), trust your hands; they'll know what to do." As it is with matters of faith, if language fails in our accounting of suffering and salvation, let our bodies speak.[44]

Studies on trauma suggest that a potential way to heal in the afterburn of violence is to give actual traumatic events symbolic meaning and representation in ways that disturb an otherwise unaffected social imaginary.[45] It is striking how the witness of these protesting bodies in Ferguson—seemingly unruly, disorderly, unfocused, even incoherent—may have facilitated a healthy process of trauma, and in doing so, served as implements for public instruction. Without their ecstatic, even hysteric, speech-act reclamation of signification—the insistence that these are the people's streets, that young Black lives are sacred, that bloody grounds

---

Theological Seminary. A recent documentary titled *Whose Streets?* chronicles the protest movement of Ferguson. See www.whosestreets.com.

43. See Francis, *Ferguson & Faith*, chap. 4.

44. Walton, *Writing Methods in Theological Reflection*, 147.

45. Charles Taylor, *Modern Social Imaginaries*, Public Planet Books (Durham, NC: Duke University Press, 2004); cited in Jeffrey C. Alexander et al., eds., *Cultural Trauma and Collective Identity* (Berkeley, CA: University of California Press, 2004); Walton, *Writing Methods in Theological Reflection*, 146.

are holy grounds—public conscience remains unscathed by the horror of suffering.[46]

We know well that many hearts remain unmoved by such catalyzing events. Nevertheless, our communities of faith persist in teaching redemptively, teaching toward individual transformation and social renewal,[47] in order to "personify"[48] the *kerygma*, the good news that all Christians have been summoned to proclaim through word and deed: "Don't be afraid. The realm of God is at hand. The world is becoming all new. It is our turn to act. 'We have nothing to lose but our chains.'"[49]

---

46. Jeffrey C. Alexander, "Toward a Theory of Cultural Trauma," in *Cultural Trauma and Collective Identity*, ed. Jeffrey C. Alexander, et al. (Berkeley, CA: University of California Press, 2004), 10–11.

47. Wexler, *Holy Sparks: Social Theory, Education, and Religion*, 142. We discuss Wexler's notion of "redemptive teaching" in chap. 6.

48. See Harvey Cox's fourfold dimensions of social change, as delineated in *The Secular City: Secularization and Urbanization in Theological Perspective* (New York: Macmillan, 1965).

49. This last line of a popular protest chant, heard ubiquitously throughout the #Ferguson and #BlackLivesMatter actions, is attributed to the Black civil rights activist Assata Olugbala Shakur.

Chapter 2
*Dis*Imagination Land

Depending upon one's calculus, the twentieth century was either the most murderous or increasingly more peace-seeking than previous eras of modern history.[1] Yet in the wake of mass shootings, deadly encounters between law enforcement and unarmed citizens, and escalating terror attacks in the United States and around the globe, it is hard to ignore the violent tantrums of the first decade and a half of the twenty-first century. Even with a sketchy memory, one can catalogue ad nauseam repetitions of violence in intricate forms both visible and invisible, and on scales both micro and macro: gun and gang violence; sexualized violence; intimate partner violence; violence motivated by religion, ethnicity, nationality (from genocide to hate crimes to acts of terror); the violence of historic and continuous injuries configured by race, gender, class, sexual orientation; state-sponsored, military violence; spiritual, psychological violence; violent acts against self; the "normalized" cultural violence found in sports, hazing, bullying; the violence of microaggressions and vitriolic rhetoric prevalent on social media and in public, political discourse; the tacit violence of unstable economies; the quiet rage imbedded in prison industrial complexes; the slow yet lethal violence of biodestruction, or ecocide.

1. Cf. Ursula King, "Reflections on Peace, Women, and the World's Faiths," *Dialogue & Alliance* 25, no. 1 (2011); Steven Pinker, *The Better Angels of Our Nature: Why Violence Has Declined* (New York: Viking, 2011). This introductory paragraph is an expansion of what I had composed, in the capacity of program chair, for the call for papers for the 2014 Annual Meeting of the Religious Education Association, the theme for which was "Religion and Education in the (Un)Making of Violence."

Most Christian faith communities are quick to condemn violence—that is, when we can actually recognize and agree on what constitutes violence. Whether or not we like to admit, modern societies deem some of the above forms of violence legitimate, acceptable, "normal." Three observations reveal the complicated nature of this moral dilemma. First, many of us think we know what violence is, and that it is deplorable; however, on both counts we often deceive ourselves. As anthropologist Jack Eller puts it, "Some [violence] we censure, some we commit ambivalently, and some we openly celebrate"[2]—for example, the execution of an enemy of the state, the exhibition of violent aggression in sports, the institutionalized violence of prison complexes, the structured violence of military warfare. Thus, even before we could venture to ask how violence can be stopped, it is necessary to ask, How do societies decide which forms of violence are objectionable and which are acceptable? Second, there is the prevailing generalization that violence is what *bad* people do to *good* people (and we can hardly imagine ourselves to be among the bad kind), but in reality, "any of us can, and many of us will" participate in some form of violence in our lifetime.[3] Third, no matter where we stand on the nature vs. nurture debate, it is hard to deny that violence is relative, relational, contextual, situational, and—most intriguing for me as an educator—it is *learned*.[4]

Social constructionists have long argued that violence is not an innate or inherent feature of human behavior but learned.[5] And because it is learned, it is also *taught*. The case to be made is this: whether its form is personal or collective hate, conflict, aggression, violation, occupation, or decimation, and whether its valence is aggressive or slow, visible or invisible, obfuscated or outrageous, deafening or quiet, violence is taught and learned in society through public pedagogies of entwined socio-culturo-

2. Jack David Eller, *Cruel Creeds, Virtuous Violence: Religious Violence across Culture and History* (Amherst: Prometheus Books, 2010), 11.

3. Ibid.

4. "Violence is a learned behavior," Tio Hardiman, former street hustler turned violence interrupter in the documentary *The Interrupters* (2011). Eller, *Cruel Deeds, Virtuous Violence,* 16.

5. James Waller, *Becoming Evil: How Ordinary People Commit Genocide and Mass Killing* (Oxford: Oxford University Press, 2002).

religious systems and practices that normalize violence in everyday life. This is not to suggest that religion and culture are inherently violent. Rather, it is to ask, Is it possible to trace the ways in which the undergirding logics of violence are being taught and learned through what we would recognize as explicit, implicit, and null curricula[6]—that is to say, forms that are expressly obvious; forms that are tacit, hidden, embedded; and forms that teach through their absence? To be sure, the roots of any form of violence reach deep into social structures, policies, and legislations, and are not just anchored by particular sets of beliefs, attitudes, and behaviors that one could easily root out and unlearn. However, in focusing inquiry on the multilayered, interstructured matrix[7] of public pedagogies that buttress the logics of violence, we better understand how or why violent ideologies and practices become normalized to our way of life. Religious educators may then reckon with our task of exposing these public pedagogies of violence, and confessing our complicity in its implementation.

Violence's Pedagogic Roots

To embark on exposing public pedagogies of violence and our complicity in implementing them, we must first ask, What do we mean by *violence*?

The study of violence across academic fields and disciplines is expansive—the Harry Frank Guggenheim Foundation is a helpful starting point for references and resources.[8] Key theological and educational definitions have contributed to the field of study. The late public theologian Robert McAfee Brown offered this take: "Whatever 'violates' another, in the sense of infringing upon or disregarding or abusing or denying [the personhood of] that other, whether physical harm is involved or not, can be understood as an act of violence."[9] With a "built-in logic and rationality," writes

6. Elliot W. Eisner, *The Educational Imagination: On the Design and Evaluation of School Programs*, 2nd ed. (New York London: Macmillan ; Collier Macmillan, 1985).

7. An expression by Christian Womanist ethicist Emilie Townes. See http://rsn.aarweb.org/spotlight-on/theo-ed/intersectionality/making-way-together.

8. The Harry Frank Guggenheim Foundation, www.hfg.org/.

9. Robert McAfee Brown, *Religion and Violence*, 2nd ed. (Philadelphia: Westminster Press, 1987), 6. See also Elizabeth T. Vasko, "Lgbt Bullying at the Crossroads of Christian Theology: Girard, Surrogate Victim, and Sexual Scapegoating," in *Violence, Transformation,*

Gabriel Moran, violence is force that "violate[s], harm[s], or destroy[s]."[10] In the language of Hannah Arendt, violence is deployed through a variety of implements and technologies.[11] Christian womanist ethicist Cheryl Kirk-Duggan amplifies the potency of violence's passive forms—the violence of *non-action*: "Ignoring the rights of another person, desensitizing oneself by observing more violent acts, and the rationalization and justification of personal or systemic use of damaging thoughts, words, or deeds is violent activity."[12] Professor of theology and ethics Fernando Enns affirms the need to keep definitions expansive. For him, violence is "physical or psychological acts of denying, injuring, or destroying human persons—their freedom of choice, their integrity, their dignity . . . denial of community . . . [and] right relationships . . . damage to nature or its destruction."[13] Feminist process theologian Marjorie Suchocki notes concisely that "at its base, violence is the destruction of well-being."[14] Putting it all together, we arrive at this conception of violence: whether passive or active, intra- or interspecies, instantaneous or intergenerational (and even intermillennial), violence is a *distortion of the sacred vitality and intimacies* of bodies, of communities, of social structures, and of earthly habitats.[15]

From these descriptive attempts, three features of violence can be extracted. *First*, violence is the violation of the vitality that is sacred and

---

and the Sacred: "They Shall Be Called Children of God," ed. Margaret R. Pfeil and Tobias L. Winright, The Annual Publication of the College Theology Society (Maryknoll: Orbis Books, 2012).

10. Gabriel Moran, *Living Nonviolently: Language for Resisting Violence* (Lanham, MD: Lexington Books, 2011), 8–9.

11. Hannah Arendt, *On Violence* (New York: Harcourt, 1970).

12. Cheryl A. Kirk-Duggan, *Misbegotten Anguish: A Theology and Ethics of Violence* (St. Louis, MO: Chalice Press, 2001), 21.

13. Fernando Enns, "Towards an Ecumenical Theology of Just Peace at the Conclusion of the 'Decade to Overcome Violence': Churches Seeking Reconciliation and Peace, 2001–2010," in *After Violence: Religion, Trauma and Reconciliation*, ed. Andrea Bieler, Christian Bingel, and Hans-Martin Gutmann (Leipzig: Evangelische Verlagsanstalt, 2011), 211.

14. Marjorie Suchocki, *The Fall to Violence: Original Sin in Relational Theology* (New York: Continuum, 1994), 85.

15. Cf. Kathleen J. Greider, *Reckoning with Aggression: Theology, Violence, and Vitality* (Louisville, KY: Westminster John Knox Press, 1997).

intimate to one's being and one's relations in and to the world. For human beings, it is a violation of personhood. Beyond anthropocentrism, violence is a violation of "essential aliveness and life-affirmation."[16] Yet violence describes not just instances of harm that we can recognize in the moment, for the violation of vitality can occur over time, at glacial speed, yet with irreparable damage. The harm cuts to the intimate core of a being's essential aliveness.

Second, violence is sustained by built-in logics. It is always accompanied by rationalization, from crude to complex ways to either justify or explain away its implementation. We are wrong when we consider acts of violence—regardless of magnitude—to be "thoughtless." Anthropologist Jack Eller posits six variables or dimensions that activate violence between individuals, groups, and species: instinct, integration (into groups), identity, institutions, interests, and ideology.[17] Together they justify harm:

> A human needs only a belief system that teaches that he or she is acting for a good reason (even a "higher cause"), under someone else's authority, as a member of a (threatened) group, in pursuit of interest. Along the way, if the individual can *learn*, by way of graduate escalation, to commit violence against someone who is worth *less*—or completely worthless, less than a human being—then violence becomes not only possible but likely, if not certain.[18]

This logic is frightening: that human beings can teach each other that it is "right" and "for good cause" to violate the essential aliveness of another, if we believe that it is done to protect what we fear we might lose, and especially if we consider the other to be worth *less* than we. This logic is not exclusive to either side of an ideological divide. In US political rhetoric, both the Left and the Right can produce systems of rationalization to explain why the opposition is worth*less*, and therefore deserving of termination. All you need is graduated escalation[19] or a "precipitating event," as Ann

16. Ibid., 9.

17. Eller, *Cruel Creeds, Virtuous Violence*, 19.

18. Ibid., 44. Emphasis added.

19. Waller, *Becoming Evil*, 232–34.

Collins calls it in her extensive study of race riots.[20] For the intricacies of motivations above, Eller defines violence as "harm that we do not approve of."[21] After all, we are less likely to condemn actions that serve our interest.

Third, violence is most potent when it is felt, not seen. Political scientist and provocateur Samuel P. Huntington capitalized on this point: "The architects of power in the United States must create a force that can be felt but not seen. Power remains strong when it remains in the dark; exposed to the sunlight it begins to evaporate."[22] Hannah Arendt famously described this stealth power as the "banality of evil"[23]; Edward Said dubbed it as "the normalized quiet of unseen power."[24] South African professor of missiology Tinyiko Sam Maluleke notes, "Violence is at its deadliest when it does not speak in its own name; the time when it hides in apparently benign policies, in culture, structures, in traditions, in 'the rule of law' and in 'law and order.'"[25] Hidden in plain sight, the stealth force of violence deals lethal blows when least expected. It is abetted by a combination of embedded socio-cultural implements, or habits and norms. It is for this reason that we must trace violence to deep, intertwining roots.

Together, these three features of violence—the erosion of essential vitality, rationalized by normalizing built-in logics, and delivered with potent force seen and unseen—bring us to a conceptual question for educators of religious and public concerns: *What are violence's pedagogic roots?* Translated, what are the public pedagogies that provide our rationalization and legitimization for the violation of individual, social, and planetary vitality?

---

20. Ann V. Collins, *All Hell Broke Loose: American Race Riots from the Progressive Era through World War II*, Praeger Series on American Political Culture (Santa Barbara, CA: Praeger, 2012).

21. Eller, *Cruel Creeds, Virtuous Violence*, 13.

22. Henry A. Giroux, *The Violence of Organized Forgetting: Thinking beyond America's Disimagination Machine*, City Lights Open Media (San Francisco: City Lights Books, 2014), 156.

23. Hannah Arendt, *Eichmann in Jerusalem: A Report on the Banality of Evil* (New York: Viking Press, 1963).

24. Rob Nixon, *Slow Violence and the Environmentalism of the Poor* (Cambridge, MA: Harvard University Press, 2011), 6.

25. Tinyiko Sam Maluleke, "After Violence, (No) More Violence? A South African Perspective," in Bieler, Bingel, and Gutmann, *After Violence*, 23.

*Dis*imagination Land[26]

To pursue this question, let us return to a present situation[27]—to that space-time that has become paradigmatic for the United States in current events. August 9, 2014, will be catalogued among the numerous dates of infamy for this country, the day on which White police officer Darren Wilson fatally shot eighteen-year-old African American Michael Brown, and the latter's body was left lifeless on a quiet suburban street of Ferguson, Missouri, for approximately four and a half hours—a dead body eerily becoming its own roadside memorial for all to see.

What happened in Ferguson was *not* the first time, nor the last, that this nation was emotionally and intellectually choked by incomprehensible violence traceable to what W. E. B. Du Bois famously dubbed the "color line" (or, in the plural, "color line*s*"); nor was it the first time we were confounded by the omnipresence of state-sanctioned, militarized enforcement of law and security; nor the first time public imagination was stumped by distorted categorization of "citizen" and "enemy combatant," "human" and "demon";[28] nor the first time we were embroiled in fiery debates about the slow violence of pervasive, structuralized, racialized inequalities and privilege. In truth, the death of young Mike Brown was but the latest paradigmatic event[29] that exposes the three characteristics

26. This is the title of a song composed by seminarian Eric Moeller, who wrote the piece in response to the reading of Henry Giroux's work.

27. We begin with the "present situation" to follow to religious education theorist Thomas Groome's "shared praxis" hermeneutic circle. Thomas H. Groome, *Christian Religious Education: Sharing Our Story and Vision* (San Francisco: Harper & Row, 1980).

28. In his testimony to the grand jury, Darren Wilson said that Michael Brown looked like a "demon." Sabrina Siddiqui, "Darren Wilson Testimony: Michael Brown Looked Like 'a Demon,'" November 25, 2014, *The Huffington Post*, http://www.huffingtonpost.com/2014/11/25/darren-wilson-testimony_n_6216620.html.

29. In another space and for other purposes, one could imagine making a case that the shooting death of Michael Brown, broadcasted via social media on live television, triggered a paradigm shift in US social imaginary. The event is "paradigmatic" in the sense developed by Garrett Green, who, following the work of Thomas S. Kuhn, proposed the concept of "paradigmatic imagination." A "paradigm" is defined as that "constitutive pattern according to which something is organized as a whole-in-parts" (52); "a normative model for a human endeavor or object of knowledge, the exemplar or privileged analogy that shows us what the object is *like*" (54, emphasis in text). Michael Brown's shooting death may have congealed

of violence delineated earlier: a violation of essential aliveness and life-affirmation; rationalized and legitimized by built-in logics; and abetted by a variety of instruments, the most potent of which remain unseen. It is a paradigmatic event that suggests US society is in the thick of what cultural theorists such as Antonio Gramsci and Stuart Hall have termed *conjuncture*: "a period in which different elements of society come together to produce a unique fusion of the economic, social, political, ideological, and cultural in relative settlement that becomes hegemonic in defining reality."[30] In pedagogic terms, it is a moment in which a new paradigm of public pedagogy is in full force—Henry Giroux labels it the "*dis*imagination machine," and it runs on the logics of neoliberal politics.

Giroux's acerbic critiques can be found in his most recent installment, *The Violence of Organized Forgetting: Thinking beyond America's Disimagination Machine.* Borrowing the concept from the work of French philosopher Georges Didi-Huberman, Giroux asserts, "A politics of disimagination has emerged, in which stories, images, institutions, discourses, and other modes of representation are undermining our capacity to bear witness to a different and critical sense of remembering, agency, ethics, and collective resistance."[31]

The implements of this *dis*imagination machine are "a set of cultural apparatuses"—public pedagogies—that "short-circuit the ability of individuals to think critically, imagine the unimaginable, and engage in thoughtful and critical dialogue, or, put simply, to become critically engaged citizens of the world."[32]

---

in the social consciousness of many a stark paradigm of reality which they could no longer deny—a pattern of lethal mistreatment of Black lives, which exemplifies countless other forms of enduring social neglect. The event may have also ushered in a paradigm shift for some, those who were jolted into recognition of a new pattern of reality that they could not "un-see" (irreversible), and a new pattern that does not cohere (incommensurate) with heretofore hoped-for notions of racial justice and equity in post-civil rights US America. See Garrett Green, *Imagining God: Theology and the Religious Imagination* (Grand Rapids: W. B. Eerdmans Pub. Co., 1998), 52, 54, emphasis in text.

30. Giroux, *The Violence of Organized Forgetting*, 45.

31. Ibid., 26–27.

32. Ibid., 27.

According to Giroux, in this conjuncture, the democratic values of individual rights—or, as Gabriel Moran would insist, *human* rights—and social accountability are eroded by "dollarocracy," masked structural disparities and depression, and "organized irresponsibility."[33] Public schools operate like "youth control complexes,"[34] in which punitive pedagogies are exercised, lockdown drills are practiced, textbooks are "White-washed" (even blatantly Christianized to the tune of conservative fundamentalism), and the creative arts are anesthetized. In socially economically stigmatized neighborhoods, schools are toxic incubators for routinized, ritualized violence,[35] and serve as a pipeline for the nation's prison industrial complex.[36] Our neighborhoods are literally either gated zones or combat zones, in which some of us are gripped by manufactured fear of intrusion by the other, and others of us are gripped by actual fear of unrelenting and debilitating surveillance and criminalization. Paramilitary equipment and tactics on the streets of Ferguson reveal the shroud of manipulated terror that is the new normal in wider cultural consciousness—a petrification of critical thinking that "[leaves] the public no option other than to trade civil liberties for increased militarized security."[37] Bodies writhing on the ground serve as a new *marturion*,[38] a public witness to the social deaths suffered by innumerable categories of persons and communities, under a form of state-abetted "intellectual violence,"[39] or public rationalizations of the legitimacy of their demise. With this form of distorted "calculus of

33. Ibid., 63, 73.

34. Ibid., 190.

35. Bowen Paulle, *Toxic Schools: High-Poverty Education in New York and Amsterdam*, Fieldwork Encounters and Discoveries (Chicago: University of Chicago Press, 2013).

36. See Michelle Alexander, *The New Jim Crow: Mass Incarceration in the Age of Colorblindness* (New York: New Press/Distributed by Perseus Distribution, 2010).

37. Giroux, *The Violence of Organized Forgetting*, 138.

38. Dale T. Irvin, "The Terror of History and the Memory of Redemption: Engaging the Ambiguities of the Christian Past," in *Surviving Terror: Hope and Justice in a World of Violence*, ed. Victoria Lee Erickson and Michelle Lim Jones (Grand Rapids: Brazos Press, 2002), 43.

39. Giroux, *The Violence of Organized Forgetting*, 104.

signification,"[40] marked bodies are downgraded/degraded to "worth less," eventually "worthless,"[41] and therefore disposable.[42]

We learn a new thanatourism—dark tourism—or thana-voyeurism: Canfield Drive, Ferguson, as ground zero for that violent outbreak, became as titillating for public viewing as the "carnival of cruelty"[43] that is enjoyed in the commercialized entertainment of films, video games,[44] or the virtual reality of online games like Second Life. It is easy to become voyeurs of violence while anesthetized to the palpability of what political theorist Achille Mbembe calls "necropolitics" and "necropower," defined as

> the various ways in which, in our contemporary world, weapons [not just police or military, but also economic, social, political, cultural] are deployed in the interest of maximum destruction of persons and the creation of *death-worlds*, new and unique forms of social existence in which vast populations are subjected to conditions of life conferring upon them the status of *living dead*.[45]

Thus, the violence of this paradigmatic event was not just a shooting death, nor the riots that ensued when civilians and law enforcement struggle to keep peace. Rather, the violence of this paradigmatic event is a cluster of (sub)urban municipalities that has become a death world for many of its residents.

Even before Michael Brown's shooting, a research team led by Dr. Jason Q. Purnell of the Warren Brown School of Social Work at Washington University in St. Louis conducted a widely heralded multidisciplinary study, "For the Sake of All," to survey the state of health and well-being

---

40. Willie James Jennings, *The Christian Imagination: Theology and the Origins of Race* (New Haven: Yale University Press, 2014), ebook edition, chap. 1.

41. Eller, *Cruel Creeds, Virtuous Violence*, 44.

42. See Henry A. Giroux, *Disposable Youth, Racialized Memories, and the Culture of Cruelty: Framing 21st Century Social Issues* (New York: Routledge, 2012).

43. Giroux, *The Violence of Organized Forgetting*, 123, 88.

44. *Call of Duty* and *Modern Warfare* are two examples of extremely popular video games that simulate strategic violent extermination of caricatured enemies.

45. Achille Mbembe, "Necropolitics," *Public Culture* 15 (2003): 40. Emphasis added.

of African Americans in greater St. Louis.[46] The research yielded a comprehensive report detailing statistical evidence of health factors and risks that correlate health status with social, economic, educational conditions. Released in May 2014, the report gave data to what many had already intuited. That is, compared to Whites, African Americans in St. Louis have higher percentages of chronic diseases (heart disease, diabetes, and certain cancers) and chronic disease risk factors; higher rates for hospitalization and emergency room visits; higher percentages of adults (ages 18–64) without health insurance and primary care; higher percentages of inadequate prenatal care; higher infant death rates and lower birth weights; higher rates of hospitalization compared to Whites for mental health care (64 percent), with some residents reporting that "violence, jail, or psychosis" are means to secure access to mental healthcare;[47] higher rates of STD (sexually transmitted disease) and HIV; and higher homicide death rates (twice as high in 2011). They make up less than 30 percent of the regional population, but 61 percent of residents in correctional facilities. In the language that adherents of dollarocracy might understand, "in one year alone, the loss of life associated with low levels of education and poverty among African Americans was estimated at $4.0 billion."[48]

Addressing statistical rates of crime-related violence, the report cites the work of the Chicago-based organization Cure Violence, founded by Gary Slutkin, MD, with its public health approach to violence prevention:

> Not just individual behavior, but the health, social, and environmental conditions that are associated with violence also must be addressed. In this way the public health approach to violence is also similar to the response to infectious diseases like tuberculosis, small pox, and polio. By understanding how violence is "transmitted" in a community, we can take steps to prevent it.[49]

46. "For the Sake of All," (St. Louis: Washington University in St. Louis, 2015). The report is downloadable at https://forthesakeofall.org/. Ferguson is one of ninety municipalities of St. Louis County.

47. Ibid., 61.

48. Errata to "For the Sake of All," 1.

49. "For the Sake of All," 62. "Cure Violence is a teaching, training, research and assessment NGO focused on a health approach to violence prevention. The Cure Violence health model is used by more than 50 cities and organizations in the U.S., as well as eight countries

If violence is the worst communicable disease, as Slutkin suggests, then a violent outbreak is only symptomatic of chronic systemic infection. The *dis*imagination machine would have us stare at some smoking gun as the piece of singled-out evidence for targeted outrage—for example, a "thuggish" Black teenager, a racist White cop, a corrupt court, a biased police chief. It is easier to rail against just one thing than to confront an ominous death world in which all of us are plagued citizens, and some of us are dying more rapidly than the rest.

Giroux calls out the *dis*imagination machine for its potent and stealthy *mis*educative power: this machine distorts the long arc of historical memory; it suffocates critical thinking and critical self-reflection; it paralyzes difficult, dissenting, divergent dialogue; it chips away moral courage and social agency; it debilitates strategies of political resistance, thereby snuffing out possibilities for "educated hope."[50] To unpack these pedagogies, we turn to one form of violence undergirding the Ferguson event, a form that has plagued the United States since its very founding: the violence of racial animus.

The Violence of Racism

In the third edition of their classic text *Racial Formation in the United States*, Michael Omi and Howard Winant expand their analysis of the social construction of race by suggesting that "*race is a master category*—a fundamental concept that has profoundly shaped, and continues to shape, the history, polity, economic structure, and culture of the United States."[51] Recognizing full well the nature of intersectionality, Omi and Winant do not regard race as transcending other markers of social identity. Rather, they maintain that given its "unique role in the formation and historical development" of this country, "race has become the *template* of both difference and inequality" in the United States, "a fundamental organizing

ranging from Canada to South Africa to Syria." From Cure Violence, accessed July 8, 2015, http://cureviolence.org/the-model/about-us/.

50. Giroux, *The Violence of Organized Forgetting*, 60, 83.

51. Michael Omi and Howard Winant, *Racial Formation in the United States*, 3rd ed. (New York: Routledge/Taylor & Francis Group, 2015), 106. Emphasis in text.

principle of social stratification."[52] The social construction of race—or the "process of race making"—is what they term *racial formation*, defined as "the sociohistorical process by which racial identities are created, lived out, transformed, and destroyed."[53] Omi and Winant's racial formation theory unfolds with valuable analytic concepts: *racialization* ("the extension of racial meaning to a previously racially unclassified relationship, social practice, or group"[54]); *racial projects* ("the simultaneous and co-constitutive ways that racial meanings are translated into social structures and become racially signified"[55]); and the problem of *racism* (when a racial project "creates or reproduces structures of domination based on racial significations and identities"[56]). This last point is instructive, for Omi and Winant submit that "race and racism are not the same thing."[57]

An educational approach to delineating the structures of racism can be found in the work of Lee Anne Bell, Michael S. Funk, Khyati Joshi, and Marjorie Valdivia, in their contribution to the third edition of a key anthology on social justice education (SJE), *Teaching for Diversity and Social Justice*.[58] There, the authors define racism as "a pervasive system of advantage and disadvantage based on the socially constructed category of

52. Ibid., 106–7.

53. Ibid., 109.

54. Ibid., 111.

55. Ibid., 109.

56. Ibid., 128.

57. Ibid., 127. We learn from Omi and Winant that the German physician and sexologist Magnus Hirschfeld—"an early advocate of gay and transgender rights"—"gave currency to the term 'racism'" in his book *Rassismus*, which "provided a history, analysis, and critical refutation of Nazi racial doctrines." Ibid., 127–28. Pushing further on the theorizing of racial formation, Omi and Winant suggest that the United States has, for most its existence, operated as a racial despotism. It is an exercise of racial dominance what allows for the "American" identity to be defined as White, and inherently "the negation of racialized 'otherness'"; it organizes social division along the "color line"; at the same time, it also yields the emergence of racial consciousness and resistance. In their view, through slow and painful struggle, most notably through the partial victories of the civil rights era, despotism may have given way to democracy, yet racial domination has morphed into the rule of racial hegemony—a totalizing exercise of control by the dominant majority, yet with both strategic and coopted consent of those who exist under their power. Ibid., 131.

58. Maurianne Adams, Lee Anne Bell, and Pat Griffin, *Teaching for Diversity and Social Justice*, 3rd ed. (New York: Routledge, 2016).

race."[59] Their instructional guide for the teaching of racial justice thoroughly covers key understandings of race and racism. They helpfully catalogue terminologies that depict the polyvalence of racist projects: individual/personal racism; institutional racism; society/cultural racism; overt racism; covert racism; racial microaggressions; internalized racism; stereotype threat; internalized dominance; unearned racial advantage/privilege; White supremacy; collusion; colorblindness.[60] They also guide us through important themes and issues that lay bare racism's intersectionality:[61] racial categorization and hierarchy; race and the regulation of immigration; citizenship and exclusion; racial classification and census categories; biracial/multiracial identities; colorism and color hierarchy; the shifting color line; linguicism and linguistic profiling.[62]

In their comprehensive overview, Bell, Funk, Joshi, and Valdivia underscore two concurrent racial projects that sustain racism's temporal and spatial endurance. The first is what critical race theorists ("crits") such as Richard Delgado and Jean Stefancic have called *differential racialization*—that is, the ways in which "each disfavored group in this country has been racialized in its own individual way and according to the needs of the majority group at particular times in its history."[63] The second is "the cumulative and systemic nature of white advantage."[64] This is the angle of

59. Lee Anne Bell et al., "Racism and White Privilege," in *Teaching for Diversity and Social Justice*, ed. Maurianne Adams, Lee Anne Bell, and Pat Griffin (New York: Routledge, 2016), 134.

60. Ibid., 134–39.

61. "Intersectionality is a way of understanding and analyzing the complexity in the world, in people, and in human experience." Intersectional analysis examines how "the events and conditions of social and political life at play [are] not shaped by any one factor [e.g., race, gender, class, exclusively] . . . [but reflect] many factors that [work] together in diverse and mutually influential ways." Intersectional frameworks attend to the following core themes: dynamics of transnational social inequality; power relations; relationality (as opposed to either/or options); contextuality; complexity; and social justice commitments. Patricia Hill Collins and Sirma Bilge, *Intersectionality*, Key Concepts Series (Cambridge, UK; Malden, MA: Polity Press, 2016), 25–30.

62. Bell et al., "Racism and White Privilege," 141–47.

63. Richard Delgado and Jean Stefancic, *Critical Race Theory: An Introduction*, 2nd ed. (New York: New York University Press, 2012), 77.

64. Bell et al., "Racism and White Privilege," 139.

analysis for crits who identify with a "realist" (or "materialist") school of thought, who insist on this close scrutiny of the "means by which society allocates privilege and status," normally to the advantage of Whites.[65]

Differential Racialization

Attending to this first racist project, we expose the logics that underlie ideologies of racial superiority (as reflected in White supremacy) and strategies of racial triangulation of disfavored groups. For Bell, Funk, Joshi, and Valdivia, the three driving logics are genocide, slavery, and orientalism. The logic of *genocide* rationalizes the inherent right of (White) "settlers" to take over newly "discovered" land, as well as whatever indigenous natural and cultural resources they could appropriate. The logic of *slavery* assumes "the control of black bodies for the economic gain of whites." The logic of *orientalism* builds upon a false binary between the superior West and the inferior rest of the world, thus stoking derisive fear of "foreigners" as "perpetual threat."[66] These logics "intertwine and reinforce each other," but they also operate distinctively in specific moments and contexts, resulting in very particular ways in which communities of color are variably "disfavored" and invariably pitted against one another.[67]

In the racialization of Latino/a persons (or Latinx[68]), for instance, we see the logic of genocidal colonization, which deems legitimate the historical

65. Delgado and Stefancic, *Critical Race Theory*, 21.

66. Bell et al., "Racism and White Privilege," 139–40.

67. Bell et al., "Racism and White Privilege," 140. To foreground the multiple intersecting structures of power, and thereby avoiding an essentialist and binary caricature of oppressor vs. oppressed, scholars such as Dorothy Smith and Chandra Talpade Mohanty prefer the notion of "relations of ruling." The concept invites examination of intersecting relations of power—e.g., gender, race, class, nationality, sexuality, ability, religion—and the ways society organizes or regulates ("rule") such relations in specific times and places, and toward specific ends. See Dorothy E. Smith, *The Everyday World as Problematic: A Feminist Sociology*, Northeastern Series in Feminist Theory (Boston: Northeastern University Press, 1987); Chandra Talpade Mohanty, *Feminism without Borders: Decolonizing Theory, Practicing Solidarity* (Durham, NC: Duke University Press, 2003).

68. "Latinx is the gender-neutral alternative to Latino, Latina and even Latin@." Tanisha Love Ramirez and Zeba Blay, "Why People Are Using the Term 'Latinx,'" *Huffington Post*, July 5, 2016, www.huffingtonpost.com/entry/why-people-are-using-the-term-latinx_us_57753328e4b0cc0fa136a159.

annexation and annihilation of peoples, lands, and cultures. At the same time, the logic of slavery is evident in exploitative use of brown labor for White wealth, while the logic of orientalism renders Latinx as threatening foreigners who violate US borders and jeopardize US social and economic safety.[69] When Asian Americans are heralded as a "model minority," it is inevitably a temporary patronization, usually to prove their willingness to out-White other disfavored groups. We forget that in the course of US history there have been moments of legislative exclusions, internment, and ghettoization of various Asian ethnic groups. During post-Civil War Reconstruction, the nation struggled to recalculate the rights of newly freed slaves, all the while considering replacement of slave labor with that of imported Chinese bodies, and ensuring that Native American claims to land and nationhood would be irreversibly dismantled through such legislations as the Indian Appropriation Act.[70]

When racial discourse is caught up in a false Black-White binary, the concept of differential racialization is an important reminder that the "dominant society often casts minority groups against one another to the detriment of all."[71] In recent current events, Asian Pacific Islander (API)[72] activist groups that join in solidarity with the #BlackLivesMatter movement know this well. Poised to rebut racial triangulation, these betwixt-and-between activists recognize the prevalence of divisive race-baiting that pits one minoritized group against another, to the extent that police

69. From Latinx socio-political perspectives, it was the border that crossed them. See, for instance, Josue David Cisneros, *The Border Crossed Us: Rhetorics of Borders, Citizenship, and Latina/O Identity*, Rhetoric, Culture, and Social Critique (Tuscaloosa, AL: The University of Alabama Press, 2014).

70. Delgado and Stefancic, *Critical Race Theory*, 79.

71. Ibid.

72. While *Oceanic* has become the preferred term over *Pacific Islander*, I use *API* here as it is still employed by many activist groups across the country. A more inclusive and problematizing self-reference might be *Asian/North American* (A/NA), with the solidus instead of the complicated hyphen, to follow David Palumbo-Liu's point: "As in the construction 'and/or,' where the solidus at once instantiates a choice between two terms, their simultaneous and equal status, and an element of indecidability, that is, as it at once implies both exclusion and inclusion, 'Asian/American' marks *both* the distinction installed between 'Asian' and 'American' *and* a dynamic, unsettled, and inclusive moment." David Palumbo-Liu, *Asian/American: Historical Crossings of a Racial Frontier* (Stanford: Stanford University Press, 1999), 1.

shootings of unarmed civilians have been cast primarily in terms of Black versus White opposition, eliding painful struggles of other communities of color with majority White law enforcement—and also obscuring complicated tensions between communities of color, or stymying activism efforts when the symbol of unjust law and order is represented by a brown or yellow body.[73] As social-cultural critic David Palumbo-Liu writes,

> The introjection of Asians into America has always taken place within a complex *multi*-racial dynamic—the Asian presence has historically prompted a reassessment of not only the general ideology of specificity of white America, but also of the presence of other racial minorities within American ideology.[74]

So depending on the ebb and flow of historical currents, Asian ethnic groups—sometimes undifferentiated, sometimes variegated—can be considered closer to Whites than Blacks, although they are just as "colored" as other non-Whites; occasionally, they are applauded for "out-whiting" White Americans. In mainstream racial imagination, Asian Americans are pivoted between the tropes of "yellow peril" (which peaked in the 1920s and 1930s, for obvious reasons) and "model minority" (which emerged in 1966 via mass media heralding of Japanese and Chinese American success).[75] Strategically wedged into the thick of various liberation movements—for instance, the Black Power movement of the 1960s—the model minority thesis reinforces the values of meritocracy and self-sufficiency, to prove that America is already a land of fair opportunity and equal access. Because it is perpetuated and unexamined, the thesis facilitates collective amnesia regarding robust multiethnic, and pan-Asian, coalitions in the civil rights movement. We also forget that W. E. B. Du Bois considered

73. See Jack Linshi, "Why Ferguson Should Matter to Asian-Americans," *Time*, November 26, 2014, http://time.com/3606900/ferguson-asian-americans/; Alan Feuer, "Ex-New York Officer Gets 5 Years of Probation in Fatal Brooklyn Shooting," *The New York Times*, April 19, 2016, https://www.nytimes.com/2016/04/20/nyregion/peter-liang-ex-new-york-police-officer-sentenced-akai-gurley-shooting-death-brooklyn.html; Ronald Takaki, "Culture Wars in the United States: Closing Reflections on the Century of the Colour Line," in *The Colonization of Imagination: Culture, Knowledge and Power*, ed. Jan Nederveen Pieterse and Bhikhu Parekh (London: Zed Books Ltd, 1995).

74. Palumbo-Liu, *Asian/American*, 149.

75. Ibid., 35–40.

the "color line" a transnational problem, not one encased only within the United States.[76]

Cumulative White Advantage and Colorblindness

Attending to the second racist project that accompanies differential racialization, we scrutinize the ways in which societal structures cumulatively confer "social advantages, benefits, and courtesies" to members of the dominant race.[77] It has been established that, like other racial categories, *whiteness* is a social construction.[78] It is "shifting and malleable," "normative" for the mainstream, and "valuable" for those who are granted its status.[79] United States legal history points to its contested nature—for example, Irish, Jews, and Italians were once non-Whites; and along the way, members of various racial/ethnic groups, including Japanese Americans, have appealed the courts (largely unsuccessfully) for attainment of White status.[80] The fact that whiteness remains dominant yet invisible in public consciousness allows the systems of social (interpersonal), institutional, and legislative "favors, exchanges, and courtesies" to remain obscure, disguised, and unregulated.[81] Accumulated over generations, this trove of invisible advantage sustains racialized inequity across major arenas of social life—namely health care, housing, education, the labor market, the criminal justice system (and the prison industrial complex), the media, local and national politics.[82] Not only that, it feeds the logic of colorblindness, which insists that race or color no longer matters, that we are in a post-racial society, that meritocratic access has been secured through

76. Tat-siong Benny Liew, ed. *Postcolonial Interventions: Essays in Honor of R. S. Sugirtharajah*, vol. 23, The Bible in the Modern World (Sheffield: Phoenix Press, 2009), 12.

77. Delgado and Stefancic, *Critical Race Theory*, 87.

78. For important analysis of the complexity of whiteness and how the racial category intersects with other markers of social location, see such work as Tex Sample's *Blue Collar Resistance and the Politics of Jesus: Doing Ministry with Working-Class Whites* (Nashville, TN: Abingdon Press, 2006).

79. Delgado and Stefancic, *Critical Race Theory*, 84–87.

80. See ibid., 85–86; Omi and Winant, *Racial Formation in the United States.*

81. Delgado and Stefancic, *Critical Race Theory*, 88.

82. Bell et al., "Racism and White Privilege," 147.

social and juridical reform. As though commonsensical, this attempt at *de*-racialization assumes a leveled playing field, that the structures, institutions, and ideologies of discriminatory racial projects have been appropriately dismantled such that it is possible to "not see color" as a factor of significance in determining anyone's ability to participate and flourish in democratic society. Under such optical illusion, considerations of race in social, political, or legal dealings (or any form of race-consciousness[83]) are met with accusations of "reverse racism." Colorblindness has been deemed by some to be one of the pitfalls of (neo)liberalism, and, for Omi and Winant, is evidence of deeply engrained racial hegemony:[84]

> Colorblindness allows people (mainly whites, but not only whites) to indulge in a kind of anti-racism "lite." While explicit forms of racial animus (such as hate speech) are widely condemned, policies and practices that continue to produce racially disparate outcomes are accepted and even encouraged under the guise of moving us "beyond" race and towards a truly colorblind society.[85]

This materialist[86] tracing of structural reinforcement of racial disparity and racial advantage pushes anti-racist work beyond facile adjustments of beliefs and attitudes. Racism is deeply engrained in cultural *dis*imagination, and it is entrenched in systemic structures that organize everyday life. It is important to dismantle the inequitable structures, but also to detoxify the ideologies[87] that sustain the rationalization of racial injustice.[88]

83. Omi and Winant, *Racial Formation in the United States.*

84. Ibid., 132, 256–60.

85. Ibid., 259.

86. Delgado and Stefancic, *Critical Race Theory*, 21.

87. Stephen Brookfield and John D. Holst, *Radicalizing Learning: Adult Education for a Just World*, The Jossey-Bass Higher and Adult Education Series (San Francisco, CA: John Wiley, 2011).

88. White scholars have begun to turn the spotlight on the problem of whiteness as central to pervasive White dominance. Shannon Sullivan, for instance, argues that even "good white liberals" fail to realize that "their experiences, beliefs, and behaviors"—even their "anti-racist" efforts and sentiments—are "shaped by and contribute to a white-dominated world." Attempts to distance themselves from racist ideologies—thereby ignoring the social infrastructures that buttress their advantaged livelihood—White liberals are quick to assign the problem of racism onto so-called ignorant Whites (a classist spatial distancing), or historic ancestors (a temporal distancing). Alternatively, they rush toward colorblind multicultural celebration,

Race as Political Theology

That race is an organizing principle of public life is echoed by South African social theorist David Theo Goldberg, who suggests that in contemporary (global) politics, race has become a political theology, a "self-secularization . . . of theological commitment and expression":

> Race was conceived to operate in much the way that theology does: as belief commitments or convictions, as a regime of truth, as defining what could and could not be thought, said, and done, how and what to believe, what bodies count, what behavior to promote or restrict, who belongs to the community and who not. Like religion, race embeds claims of both origin and kinship. In short, what is at issue are beliefs, bodies, and behavior, culture and character.[89]

Numerous contemporary race critics offer evocative paradigms for our partial comprehension of racism's entrenchment in US psyche.[90] Here, we want to understand racism as a spiritual concern,[91] an expression of theological *dis*imagination. Race has become an implement by which society configures valuations of origins, belonging, identity, worth. Like a political theology, race "colonizes and absolutizes belief":

> It defines who belongs, who doesn't, who's in, who's out, who has standing in the community, who does not, who's part of the community and who's

---

only to prove yet again the power of White "ontological expansiveness"—that is, "the habit, often unconscious, of assuming and acting as if any and all spaces—geographical, psychological, cultural, linguistic, or whatever—are rightfully available to and open for white people to enter whenever they like." When all else fails, good White liberals succumb to guilt and shame, and rhetorical denouncement of their own racialized identity. Shannon Sullivan, *Good White People: The Problem with Middle-Class White Anti-Racism*, Suny Series, Philosophy and Race (Albany: SUNY Press, 2014), 2, 4, 20.

89. David Theo Goldberg and Susan Searls Giroux, *Sites of Race: Conversations with Susan Searls Goroux* (Malden, MA: Polity Press, 2014), 49.

90. See, for instance, bell hooks's exposition of White pathology, or Emilie Townes's notion of "fantastical hegemonic imagination"; bell hooks, *Killing Rage: Ending Racism* (New York: H. Holt and Co., 1995); Emilie M. Townes, "Teaching and the Imagination," *Religious Education* (2016), DOI: 10.1080/00344087.2016.1191586.

91. Sullivan writes, "My concern [about White racism] is *spiritual* in that it examines what psychosomatically animates white people in their pursuit of racial justice." Sullivan, *Good White People*, 12.

> not, where the lines are drawn, how they are drawn, under what sets of definition, and how those investments become ramified into forms of antagonism, humiliation, refinement, and in some ways rupture.[92]

Goldberg's analysis of the "disfiguring of race"[93] toward racist agendas echoes the pedagogies of *dis*imagination described by Giroux. And what Giroux calls mentacide,[94] Goldberg laments as the amnesiatic and strategic erasure of the long arc of historic memory, such that instead of crime scenes Southern plantations could become "tourist attractions, white-washed museums to nostalgic make-believe."[95] What Giroux calls the suffocation of critical thinking and public dialogue is comparable to Goldberg's indictment of the invisibilization of racism: that racial conversation is now to be rendered private and personal, left to individual sentiment and judgment, and immune from government regulation.[96] In civic matters, we are to assume "racelessness," another word for colorblindness. Finally, what Giroux decries as the loss of etho-political agency, Goldberg identifies as a mistaken "god complex" of racial superiority that draws on a messianic sense of destiny.[97] The messianism affords a privilege of waiting—"a deferral, a putting off," a self-assuring "state of doing nothing," an assumption that the problem would be corrected by some deliverer someday.[98] The luxury to wait fails to see the "weight of race"[99] that crushes down on those caught in what Omi and Winant call "chronic crisis"[100]—a liminal in-between time in which "the old is dying and the new cannot be born."[101]

92. Goldberg and Giroux, *Sites of Race*, 50.

93. Ibid., 56.

94. Giroux, *The Violence of Organized Forgetting*, 192.

95. Goldberg and Giroux, *Sites of Race*, 56–57.

96. Ibid., 52, 56.

97. Ibid., 50.

98. Ibid., 60–61.

99. Ibid., 58.

100. Omi and Winant, *Racial Formation in the United States*, 9.

101. Antonio Gramsci, *Selections from the Prison Notebooks*, trans. Quintin Hoare and Geoffrey Nowell-Smith (New York: International Publishers, 1971), 276; cited in ibid.

Christian Disimagination

Goldberg's indictment of the disfiguring of race resonates strikingly with Willie James Jennings's estimation of the "diseased" Christian imagination, a "calculus of signification built around white bodies," the consequence of which is the severance of any profound sense of "belonging, connection, and intimacy" that is fundamental to the Christian understanding of incarnation.[102] With such distorted political theology of origins, belonging, identity, and worth, White European colonialists put themselves at the center of a creation story that assumed their endowed right to displacement of land, conscription of bodies, and appropriation of cultures. Part of this supersessionism is a sense of entitlement to renarrate the world order as though from scratch, *ex nihilo*.

How Christianity (d)evolved from complicated pluri-ethno-religious coexistence in the early centuries[103] to becoming an engine for hegemonic Western colonial expansion is a history too tortuous for synopsis here, but the imaginative leap one could take from one theologian's diagnosis of a diseased imagination offers a pattern of recognition for more contemporary findings by sociologists of religion who conclude that Christians today continue to organize segregated lives based on their Christian imagination.[104] In their unsettling study with white evangelicals, sociologists Michael O. Emerson and Christian Smith presented empirical data to suggest that it is their foundational theological toolkits that prevent this demographic of faithfuls from recognizing the insidiousness of systemic racism. The theological undercurrents of divine election and destiny buttress a peculiar configuration of identity and vocation in which the Christian, endowed with individual freewill, is responsible for their own salvation. As Emerson and Smith observed, in this theo-ethical paradigm, the problem of race is understood as a problem of personal sin—the sin of individual prejudice, which could easily be overcome with earnest re-

102. Jennings, *The Christian Imagination*, ebook edition, introduction and chap. 1.

103. See Marion Grau, *Rethinking Mission in the Postcolony: Salvation, Society and Subversion* (London: T&T Clark, 2011).

104. Michael O. Emerson and Christian Smith, *Divided by Faith: Evangelical Religion and the Problem of Race in America* (Oxford: Oxford University Press, 2000).

pentance and goodwilled relations.[105] The trouble with this soteriological construct is that one cannot repent from that which one does not recognize or is unable to acknowledge.

Emerson and Smith propose that the US religious landscape is analogous to a marketplace, in which the ideals of choice, variety, competition, and niche marketing configure group identities and boundaries.[106] One suspects that this marketplace is powered by the political economics of neoliberal capitalism and self-affirmative meritocracy. Under the illusion of free choice, individuals are wired to *mis*recognize what the researchers call the homophily principle—that we are more likely to forge social relations with people who are "like us" than with people who seem sociodemographically different from us.[107] The stability and cost-effectiveness of "internally similar" groupings—and Christian congregations are one such type of internally similar organization—yield a social configuration in which goodwill relations with those different and therefore distant from us are structurally challenging, if not unimaginable. Religious groupings remain racially homogenous, the religious market is segmented, similarities and differences among groups become exaggerated to feed "ingroup bias."[108] With a macro view, we are taken aback by how the organization of religious communities "contributes to [the] consolidation along racial lines."[109] The indictment is brutal, and not just for White evangelicals: "Religion, in the context of a racialized society, accentuates group boundaries, divisions, categorizations, and the biases that follow."[110]

105. Ibid., 78, 88.

106. Ibid., 136, 43.

107. Ibid., 147.

108. In his book *Becoming Evil,* social psychologist James Waller uses as case studies instances of genocide and mass killings around the globe, to extrapolate models that explain why ordinary people could possibly engage in extraordinary evil. One particular set of dynamics is illuminating: his proposition that "social death of the victim" is facilitated by the entwined logics of "us vs. them" (in which essentialized sameness is accentuated for biased social classification); dehumanization (from hyper-differentiating difference, to linguistic dehumanization, to physical "machination" of the other); and "blame the victim" (on a "just world scale," we are "good" and the other is "bad"). See Waller, *Becoming Evil,* chapter 7.

109. Emerson and Smith, *Divided by Faith,* 153–57.

110. Ibid., 158.

Why Is Racism a Form of Violence?

Racism is readily condemned by religious liberals as a form of social injustice, and by their evangelical counterparts as an insidious taint of original sin.[111] Here, we cast racism as a form of violence of which every member of society is an active producer, even as some of us are simultaneously victims of its ongoing production. If violence is defined by the three characteristics presented earlier in this chapter—the erosion of essential vitality, rationalized by normalizing built-in logics, and delivered with potent force seen and unseen—then we might appreciate the severity of racism as a form of violence. For starters, our seemingly benign affinity for sameness yields an increased "distance spectrum"[112] between self and the dissimilar other. With segmented existence comes an obliviousness to the reality of those outside our frame of reference—an apathy that asks, "What does that life have to do with mine?" What results (or instigates) may be a solipsism, an incapacity to take perspectives other than one's own. Exaggerated similarities and differences between "us and them" fester, almost inevitably under the presumption that we are better than they, and, subsequently, that they are a threat to us. As this gap of intimacy widens and stiffens, the worth of the other decreases—to a point where they may even become less human, sub-human, deserving of what is "justly" dealt to them.

Together, a theological system that desacralizes human affinity to one another and to their space-time, and a socio-religious system that rationalizes stratification serve as potent implements that strip the vitality of both us and them. By our diseased social imagination, the other dies a social death even before we can detect the deterioration of their physical and environmental conditions. The very ways in which we organize and practice faith are, in effect, contributing to collective *misre*cognition of "what bodies count,"[113] and *how* they count, and how they should count to *us*.

---

111. See Jim Wallis, *America's Original Sin: Racism, White Privilege, and the Bridge to a New America* (Grand Rapids: Brazos Press, 2016).

112. Waller describes various distancing strategies employed by social groups that potentially escalate from "us vs. them" thinking, to "moral disengagement," to dehumanization of the other, to blame the victim.

113. Goldberg and Giroux, *Sites of Race*, 49.

Here we turn to the enterprise of religious education for explicit problem-posing: How is the ministry of teaching and learning in Christian faith communities today complicit in the *dis*imagination machine? In our endeavors to "make accessible and make manifest"[114] the repertoires of religious stories, rituals, and ethical guides for daily meaning-making and decision-making, and even in our endeavors to draw on the best of religious resources to denounce violence explicitly, how are the programs and purposes of faith formation in our respective traditions still *colonized* by *dis*imagination in ways that run contrary to the best of our ethico-religious ideals and expressed beliefs?

With these questions, we turn to the next chapter.

114. Mary C. Boys, *Educating in Faith: Maps and Visions* (San Francisco: Harper & Row, 1989), 193.

Chapter 3

The Violence of Religious Educational Practice

Q. What is the Fifth Commandment?

A. Honour [sic] thy Father and Mother.

Q. What is the meaning of it?

A. I must show all due Respect unto Every One; and if I have a Master or Mistress, I must be very dutiful unto them.[1]

In 1706, a reprinted pamphlet attributed to the renowned New England Puritan preacher Cotton Mather, titled *A Negro Christianized,* gained wide circulation within a population of roughly ninety thousand, about one thousand of whom were slaves imported from the West Indies. In the pamphlet, the charismatic religious and political leader beseeched his fellow White colonialists to attend to the souls of their Black slaves for both spiritual and practical reasons: it is, after all, a Christian duty to save every soul; but practically speaking, a Christianized servant is a profitably domesticated one.[2] Proffering eloquent philosophical and theological rhetoric, one brief and one extended catechism, and additional instructions

1. Catechetical instructions on the Ten Commandments produced by the New England Puritan preacher of the Second (North) Church, Cotton Mather, in his widespread pamphlet *The Negro Christianized,* 28.

2. Cotton Mather, "The Negro Christianized: An Essay to Excite and Assist the Good Work, the Instruction of Negro-Servants in Christianity (1706)," ed. Paul Royster (Farmington Hills: Thomson Gale, originally published in 1706), 28; see http://digitalcommons.unl.edu/cgi/viewcontent.cgi?article=1028&context=etas.

for the teaching of the Ten Commandments, the Lord's Prayer, and other basic doctrines of the Christian faith, Mather assured Christian masters that good catechism does *not* liberate enslaved bodies:

> What *Law* is it, that Sets the *Baptised* [sic] *Slave* at *Liberty*? Not the *Law of Christianity*: that allows of Slavery; Only it wonderfully Dulcifies, and Mollifies, and Moderates the Circumstances of it. *Christianity* directs a *Slave*, upon his embracing the *Law of the Redeemer*, to satisfy himself, *That he is the Lords Free-man*, tho' he continues a *Slave*. . . . Will the *Canon-law* do it? No; . . . Will the *Civil Law* do it? No.[3]

New Testament scholar Mitzi J. Smith calls this instantiation of "slave catechism" a "sacralized pedagogy of oppression." Drawing our attention to the repertoire of early colonial American religious educational materials that emphasized the missional conversion of so-called heathens, Smith argues that

> slave masters and missionaries used slave catechisms as a means of instructing slaves in the Christian religion in order to save their *souls*. Saving black *souls* became inextricably linked with maintaining slavery and thus the continued traumatization of the black *psyche* . . . [meaning] the total human being, the lives of black folks.[4]

This history of "sacralized pedagogy of oppression" bleeds into contemporary times, as we observe innumerable instances of explicit teaching of Christian scriptures, church doctrines, and faith practices that justify hatred, bigotry, and exclusion. On one hand, it is easy to think of such extreme cases as that of the Westboro Baptist Church, an outlying religious sect that draws upon a hyper-Calvinism (of double and absolute predestination) to teach and preach hate against almost every group external to its exclusive membership.[5] On the other hand, a historical review of any

3. Mather, *The Negro Christianized*, 16–17. Emphasis in original.

4. Smith, "US Colonial Missions to African Slaves: Catechizing Black Souls, Traumatizing the Black Psychē," in *Teaching All Nations: Interrogating the Matthean Great Commission*, ed. Mitzi J. Smith and Jayachitra Lalitha (Minneapolis: Fortress Press, 2014), ProQuest ebrary, accessed September 15, 2016.

5. Rebecca Barrett-Fox, *God Hates: Westboro Baptist Church, American Nationalism, and the Religious Right* (Lawrence, KS: University Press of Kansas, 2016).

old-line Christian denomination would reveal undercurrents of similar hate- and fear-based Christian teachings.

What if, instead of being communities of good news, Christian faith communities are actually communities plagued by these enduring forms of violence? What if our enterprise of religious formation is being forged by a pervasive curriculum of violence, implemented through a variety of sacralized oppressive pedagogies, as we continue to deny or fail to recognize the insidiousness of our complicity in intersecting repressive structures throughout history and in contemporary society? What if many Christian churches are not just dying institutions but also toxic communities that actively emit symptoms of violence discussed in the previous chapter: violation of the sacred, intimate vitality of persons and creation, backed by built-in logics, dispensed through multiple implements, the most lethal of which are unseen? If we could face into this starker reality—the gravity of this death world—perhaps we might understand the urgent need for something more than quick technical fixes or nostalgic eulogies.

Adaptive Challenges of Christian Religious Education

Christian religious communities have been told in no uncertain terms that they are confronting *adaptive challenges* rather than technical difficulties—a new truism for religious leadership, thanks in large part to the work of Ron Heifetz and Marty Linksy.[6] An adaptive challenge signals the internal destabilization of a paradigm, a debilitating incongruence between larger values and visions and the day-to-day structures and operations that sustain an entity or institution. Adaptive problems are complexly interstructured and cannot be remedied through quick technical fixes. A capital campaign to maintain the operational budget of a city church with dwindling membership is a technical fix. The changing

6. See Ronald A. Heifetz and Martin Linsky, *Leadership on the Line: Staying Alive through the Dangers of Leading* (Boston: Harvard Business School Press, 2002); Ronald A. Heifetz, *Leadership without Easy Answers* (Cambridge: Belknap Press of Harvard University Press, 1994). See also Dan Aleshire's prognostication for the future of theological schools, in Daniel O. Aleshire, "The Future Has Arrived: Changing Theological Education in a Changed World," *Theological Education* 46, no. 2 (2011): 69–80.

socio-demographic of the city, the rise of poverty, crime, unemployment, economic stress, and segregated neighborhoods are adaptive challenges. The hiring of a new part-time director of "[such and such] ministries" is a technical fix. The shifting cultural and religious landscape of surrounding zip codes, with increasing diversity and polarization, are adaptive challenges.

In light of longitudinal seismic shifts in religious institutions and patterns of religious life writ large, one wonders whether the ministry of teaching and learning within Christian religious communities has sufficiently responded to the ways in which the daily values, habits, and organizational infrastructures of congregations have or have not been appropriately reconfigured in response to changing times. *Infrastructure* is used here in the sense proposed by longtime scholar of religion and education Charles F. Foster: the web of "*practices* essential to the creation and maintenance of any group or community."[7] By this, Foster means the daily habits and structures that organize a community, and the "deeply rooted patterns of meaning" shared by its people—which, according to Foster, have become deeply flawed in Christian congregations.

Foster's verdict was first presented in his 1994 volume *Educating Congregations: The Future of Christian Education*.[8] In no uncertain terms, Foster informed the Christian church of North America of the "serious threat" to its future, stating that "its education can no longer maintain its heritage into the present or renew its identity or vocation for its changing circumstances."[9] The crisis, he wrote, was one of crumbling infrastructures needed to "build up faith communities capable of incarnating Christ's ministries of love and justice appropriate to God's mission at the juncture of the twentieth and twenty-first centuries."[10] In systematic fashion, Foster laid out what he considered to be five fundamental flaws of the earthen vessel that is church education (fig. 3.1):

7. Charles R. Foster, *Educating Congregations: The Future of Christian Education* (Nashville: Abingdon Press, 1994), xv. Emphasis in text.

8. Ibid.

9. Ibid., 11.

10. Ibid., 13.

1. The loss of communal memory in congregational life
2. The irrelevance of our teaching about the Bible for contemporary life
3. The subversion of educational goals
4. The cultural captivity of church education
5. The collapse of the church's educational strategy[11]

Though articulated over twenty years ago, this diagnosis is still alarmingly relevant. So what did Foster mean by these five flaws, and how do they continue to apply today?

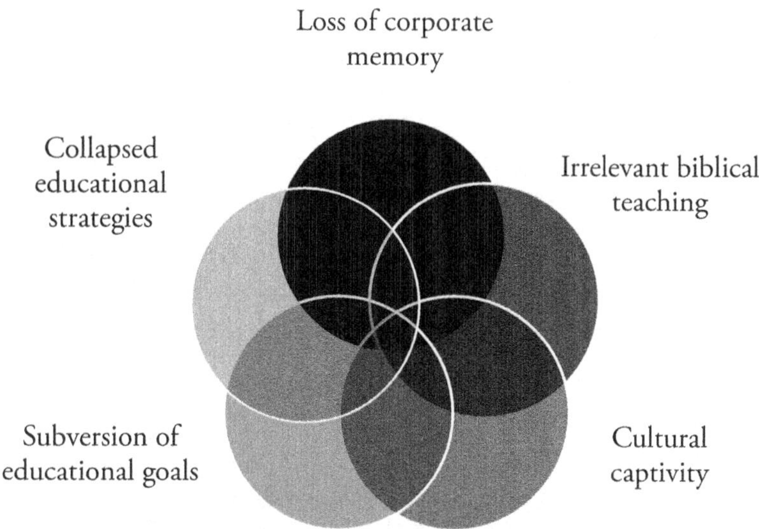

Figure 3.1 Five Flaws of the Church Educational Vessel (Charles Foster)

First, by the loss of communal or corporate memory, Foster means a growing generational disconnect facilitated by young people's eager exit from the family and the church, which at the time was part and parcel of a socially scripted mainstream rite of passage. Given his knowledge of the particularity of culture and social circumstances, Foster would be the first

11. Ibid., 22.

to amend that this drama of "spread your wings" self-discovery does not apply to youth of all socio-demographic groups. However, the generally accepted departure from home and church means that the young lose any sense of connectedness to the "ancestral traditions and experience"[12] of faith that might shape their identity and vocation as maturing adults.[13] They become "illiterate" in the language of their faith culture and tradition. *Second*, the irrelevance of biblical teaching refers to "theology-lite" approaches to teaching and learning in the church, an either naïve or arrogant anti-intellectualism that deprives smart laity of access to rich resources of biblical and theological discovery. *Third*, the educational goals of the church are subverted, in Foster's estimation, when populist needs or niche-marketing drive educational programming. Entertainment replaces discipleship for a cafeteria-styled approach to "consumption rather than transformation."[14] *Fourth*, church education surrenders to cultural captivity with its "proclivity to sanction the cultural status quo" of "racism, sexism, ageism, classism, and other 'isms' diminishing God's intentions for all people."[15] Such an implicit acceptance of societal oppressions undermines any explicit curricula of the gospel. *Finally*, with misguided intention and direction, and in uphill competition with exploding cultural attractions (media, technology, social activities), the church sees the crumbling of supporting structures that once made education strategically intercon-

12. Ibid., 24.

13. Rich literature emerged in the 1990s and 2000s on the variety of youth and young adult psycho-social developmental needs and cultural-religious experiences. A small sample of practical theological research in this regard include Dori Grinenko Baker and Joyce Mercer, *Lives to Offer: Accompanying Youth on Their Vocational Quests*, Youth Ministry Alternatives (Cleveland: Pilgrim Press, 2007); Evelyn L. Parker, *The Sacred Selves of Adolescent Girls: Hard Stories of Race, Class, and Gender* (Cleveland: Pilgrim Press, 2006); Christian Smith and Melinda Lundquist Denton, *Soul Searching: The Religious and Spiritual Lives of American Teenagers* (Oxford: Oxford University Press, 2005); Katherine Turpin, *Branded: Adolescents Converting from Consumer Faith*, Youth Ministry Alternatives (Cleveland: Pilgrim Press, 2006). An important volume that merged adolescent psychology with critical racial theory is Beverly Daniel Tatum, *"Why Are All the Black Kids Sitting Together in the Cafeteria?" And Other Conversations about Race* (New York: BasicBooks, 1997).

14. Foster, *Educating Congregations*, 29.

15. Ibid., 31.

nected between family, church, and public domains—specifically public schools.

In 2012, almost twenty years later, Foster revisited his prior appraisal with crisp new research and illustrated analysis of the adaptive challenges of mainline Protestant church education in an installment that reflects the complex simplicity of fifty years' worth of practical wisdom. In this later iteration, *From Generation to Generation: The Adaptive Challenge of Mainline Protestant Education in Forming Faith*, Foster reduces his previous list of five flaws of the church to four losses:

- The loss of reinforcing structures for educational efforts
- The loss of a catechetical culture for faith formation
- The loss of a compelling narrative about God in the crosscurrents of theological, religious, and cultural diversity
- The loss of intergenerational ties in mentoring faith formation[16]

The *first* loss is what Foster had noted previously: the breakdown of family-church-school interdependence. In this analysis, however, Foster specifically underscores the church's own relinquishing of its public voice, abandoning what some religious education scholars call its "public duty,"[17] on matters concerning the future of young people. Acquiescing to narratives of decline—and perhaps in good liberal fashion, accepting an ill-informed exercise of church-state separation—"the denominations of the old Protestant mainline abdicated responsibility for constructively critiquing the mission and strategy of the national's schools in the quest for the 'best' education for all the nation's children and youth."[18] As has been said about global Christian missional efforts, a retreat of religious liberals creates a

16. Charles R. Foster, *From Generation to Generation: The Adaptive Challenge of Mainline Protestant Education in Forming Faith* (Eugene: Cascade Books, 2012), 50. Used by permission of Wipf and Stock Publishers. www.wipfandstock.com.

17. Jack L. Seymour and Donald E. Miller, eds., *Theological Approaches to Christian Education* (Nashville: Abingdon Press, 1990), 8.

18. Foster, *From Generation to Generation*, 54.

vacuum that is quickly filled by other Christian counterparts—typically and unabashedly by more fundamentalist alternatives. Foster notes, for example, the highly contested cases of Christian fundamentalist encroachment in the selection of public school textbooks.[19]

The *second* loss, for Foster, is a breakdown of cohesive and comprehensive infrastructures for faith formation, from the grassroots level of local congregations up to the heights of judicatory bodies. Faith formation requires "catechetical cultures," Foster argues—organic yet tightly structured, expertly resourced, internally anchored, and externally supported social learning environments that facilitate the dynamic "handing down" of theological ideas, values, and practices that sustain faith.[20] The dismantling of such nurturing cultures result in the *third* loss: a theological imagination, a worldview, a reservoir—a "narrative of God"—that is robust enough for persons of faith to face boldly into a pluralistic and polarizing world. As Robert Putnam put so succinctly in his book *American Grace: How Religion Divides and Unites Us*, in the United States "religious pluralism coexist[s] with religious polarization."[21] If religious teaching and learning in churches do not power our imagination to think and act *theologically* in the realness and messiness of everyday life—especially in pluralistic spaces and polarizing situations—then our educational endeavors are for naught. For Foster, the technical evidence of this adaptive challenge is found in the ways denominations fumble in the work of curriculum development. Church publishers agonize over what would sell, isolated denominational staff struggle to translate new ideas to local levels,

19. Ibid., 51–55. See Mark A. Chancey's critical review of the conservative National Council on Bible Curriculum in Public Schools and its push for a disguised confessional approach to teaching the Bible in public school through its textbook, *The Bible in History and Literature*: Mark A. Chancey, "A Textbook Example of the Christian Right: The National Council on Bible Curriculum in Public Schools," *Journal of the American Academy of Religion* 75, no. 3 (September 2007). The NCBCPS claims to have successfully introduced its curriculum to 2,900 high schools in thirty-nine states; see National Council on Bible Curriculum in Public School, accessed September 16, 2016, http://bibleinschools.net/About-Us/.

20. Foster, *From Generation to Generation*, 55–61, 97.

21. Robert D. Putnam and David E. Campbell, *American Grace: How Religion Divides and Unites Us* (New York: Simon & Schuster, 2010), 4–6.

while leaders in congregations are left to their own devices in the work of educating for faith that matters in a changing world.[22]

The *fourth* loss in Foster's analysis are the prevailing concerns about generational gaps. Backed by contemporary research on adolescents, Foster reminds aging churches of what they may find too painful to reconcile: that the younger generations of today are neglected socially, culturally, economically, and politically. Maligned as a cohort of spiritually vagrant "nones" and "dones," Millennials and those born after them are considered fugitives in a society that continues to scapegoat them for various social ills. Double messages from grown-ups abound: young people are exhorted toward high aspirations, yet societal conditions are such that only a privileged few would be able to actualize such dreams. Youth are told they are welcomed in the church, yet they must participate according to the rules and rituals choreographed by adults.[23]

The tragic loss of young lives to violence—particularly young Black lives in violent encounters with law enforcement—leaves an afterburn on our collective psyche, beckoning religious communities toward serious reckoning with the adaptive challenges encapsulated in the systemic losses assessed by Foster. We are not just talking about a generic social demographic of free-wheeling youth who are exiting churches in search of alternative religious affiliations and experiences. Pay attention,[24] and we discover the ways in which young people are taking the lead in becoming innovators of cultural, religious, and political change—outside the walls of the church.[25]

22. Foster, *From Generation to Generation*, 62–66.

23. Ibid., 66–71.

24. A mantra in Jack Seymour's latest religious educational imperative. Jack L. Seymour, "Paying Attention: Educating for Redemptive Communities," in *Educating for Redemptive Community: Essays in Honor of Jack Seymour and Margaret Ann Crain,* ed. Denise Janssen (Eugene: Wipf and Stock, 2015).

25. Among abounding examples, one group of twenty-something activists emerged within the stream of recent grassroots freedom movements are the Millennial Activists United, MAU, in the wake of the shooting death of Michael Brown; Cheryl Corley, "With Ferguson Protests, 20-Somethings Become First-Time Activists," NPR, October 24, 2014, www.npr.org/2014/10/24/358054785/with-ferguson-protests-20-somethings-become-first-time-activists.

Religious Educational Malpractice

What if the situation is even *worse* than Foster suggests?

I would venture that the typologies of infrastructural flaws and systemic losses are useful categories for our contemplation of more devastating news for the state of predominantly White mainline—whitestream—Christian churches. It is easy to reach for Band-Aid solutions, to lean on messianic waiting, or simply to count our losses and trim our goals to modest middle-class size, if we concede that the adaptive challenges are simply part and parcel to the progress of change. Put differently, responses to tectonic structural shifts in mainline Protestant churches seem to range somewhere between fearful paralysis and entrepreneurial fits. At either end of the spectrum, the obsession is still centripetal—inwardly focused, myopically spiraling. We lament the steady erosion of the church as earthen yet sacramental vessels of the good news incarnate. We accept inevitable loss, but we believe that something pure and precious at the core is still being harnessed—some transcendent value, some enduring inheritance, some cherished habits and practices, some patterns of relationships that would eventually break forth in new forms for the church of tomorrow.

In all these ways we are deceiving ourselves. Suppose we attempt a few twists to Foster's appraisal of flaws and losses, and wake up to a verdict even starker than what good Christians are telling themselves. What if we were to take seriously the question asked at the beginning of this chapter: In what ways are Christian faith communities plagued by enduring violence, perpetuated explicitly and implicitly through forms of religious educational malpractice?

To pursue this question, let us consider the following reinterpretations of Foster's five flaws (fig. 3.2):

1. Loss of corporate memory ➡ Erasure of historical memory
2. Irrelevant biblical teaching ➡ The Bible as a weapon of mass destruction
3. Cultural captivity ➡ The church as fractured sanctuary

4. Subversion of educational goals ➡ A habitus of *dis*imagination

5. Collapse of educational strategies ➡ Banking educational curricula

Framed this way, we ponder how certain flaws of church education function as tragic curricula of violence, producing "sacralized pedagogies of oppression," to borrow Mitzi Smith's expression. The combination of these elements—purposeful erasure of historical memory, the use of the Bible as a destructive weapon, the fractured nature of community, an insidious *habitus* or logic of *dis*imagination, and the repressive practice of "banking" teaching—results in a habitat that is spiritually violent in the ways described previously: a violation of the essential aliveness of persons and creation, backed by built-in logics, dispensed through multiple implements, the most lethal of which are unseen. Let us consider each of these elements below.

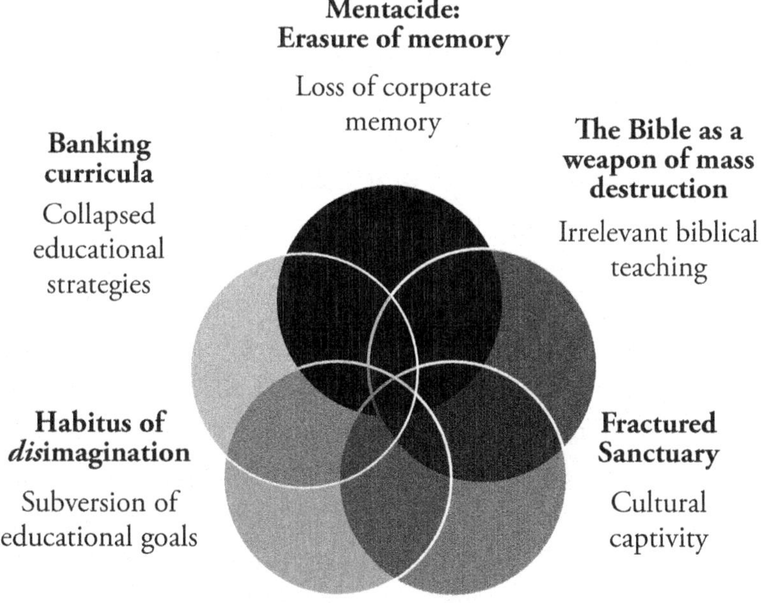

Figure 3.2 Pedagogies of Violence

Mentacide: Erasure of Historical Memory

The loss of memory, which Foster discusses may not be incidental. Memory loss can be the result of purposeful erasure. Critical educational theorist Henry Giroux calls this "the violence of organized forgetting."[26] Memory not only sustains generational wisdom, as Foster suggests; memory organizes how we live in the aftermath of violence, in the afterburn of atrocities that affect us personally and injustices that mar us socially. Unfortunately, as Giroux contends, "America—a country in which forms of historical, political, and moral forgetting are not only willfully practiced, but celebrated—has become amnesiac."[27] Powered by the *dis*imagination machine, it is a process of *mentacide*—"an erasure of historical memory," and ultimately a means of suppressing the counter-memories of marginalized peoples.[28]

The church commits mentacide when it suppresses memories of suffering and injustice. "Organized forgetting" is a fitting expression, because this type of memory loss does not occur by happenstance. In fact, it takes energy and effort to wipe some*thing* or some*one* out of existence, and also to wipe our collective memory of such deeds. Educators familiar with the typologies of explicit, implicit, and null curricula will tell us that the *null*—what is left out, what is deemed taboo, what is missing by neglect or willful forgetting—can be as potent and lethal as the explicit. Take, for example, the curricular erasure of historical memory of slave catechisms (how many church educators are aware of the existence of such "resources"?), or of a denomination's embarrassing legacy of racism. As mainline denominations like The United Methodist Church strive to live faithfully into the vision of being a culturally diverse and racially just ecclesiastical body, one wonders whether it still actively teaches members about the painful history of racial prejudice, in which prominent judicatory leaders once resisted the notion of "social equality" among the races, defended White racial supremacy, and "actively promote[d] a climate of

26. Giroux, *The Violence of Organized Forgetting.*

27. Ibid., 25.

28. Ibid., 192. Here, Giroux references the ideas of convicted activist Mumia Abu-Jamal.

racial hatred and fear."[29] Thus, while major Christian denominations have engaged in acts of liturgical confession and repentance for historic injuries caused in the name of faith—the legacies of genocide, enslavement, internment, exclusion, dehumanization, neglect—we wonder whether the memories of such injuries are ever accessed for continuous educative purposes in the daily life of the church.[30] We wonder whether church education would risk the power of "dangerous memories"—or "personal or communal memories with an endless capacity to disturb complacency

29. Morris L. Davis, *The Methodist Unification: Christianity and the Politics of Race in the Jim Crow Era* (New York: NYU Press, 2008), ebook edition, chaps. 1, 4. Writing on the tensions of race and Methodist unification in the Jim Crow era, Davis exposed deep schisms along the color line within a church body seeking Christian unity in the midst of deep-seated social segregation. Analyzing *The Proceedings of the Joint Commission on Unification of the Methodist Episcopal Church, and Methodist Episcopal Church, South*, which met between 1916 and 1920 to deliberate the conditions of a merger, Davis recounts the argument of Alexander Simpson Jr., a lay delegate to the Joint Commission and Supreme Court Justice of Pennsylvania, who laid biblical foundation for his antisocial equality stance as follows:

"Jesus might have been 'the greatest Social Democrat the world has ever known,' but he was also 'of an inferior race . . . and despised even by a conquered people.' And since Jesus did not teach or struggle for his own social equality, this was not a principle that was a product of his teaching. Jesus did not teach 'social equality, but, please God, He taught us religious equality, and not one word or act of His, so far as the Bible shows, taught anything else'" (ebook edition, chap. 4).

Chronicling the history of American Methodism, Russell Richey, Kenneth Rowe, and Jean Miller Schmidt document the irony of ecclesial attempts at segregated unification:

"Just as the nation was becoming more sensitive to its racial inequalities and to segregation as a blight on democracy, Methodism had made more visible and constitutional the color line it had long drawn within its fraternity, a step backward that southern white Methodist women clearly recognized. A united Methodism would be jurisdictioned, divided by race and region—all the African American conferences and most of its congregations gathered into one Central Jurisdiction, and white Methodism united by regions." Kenneth E. Rowe, Russell E. Richey, Jean Miller Schmidt, *The Methodist Experience in America*, vol. 1 (Nashville: Abingdon Press), ebook edition, chap. 12.

30. I am told that a forthcoming resource by David Hansen responds to this educational task; it is titled *Native Americans, The Mainline Church, and the Quest for Interracial Justice* (Chalice Press). The 2016 General Conference of The United Methodist Church devoted time for remembrance, education, and a liturgy of repentance for Methodist involvement in the 1864 Sand Creek Massacre. Soldiers of the Union Army, led by a Methodist Episcopal Church pastor, attacked a Cheyenne and Arapaho encampment and slaughtered about 200 Native Americans. See Sam Hodges, "GC2016 recalls, laments, Sand Creek Massacre," United Methodist Church, May 18, 2016, www.umc.org/news-and-media/gc2016-recalls-laments-sand-creek-massacre. This history is recounted in Gary Roberts's book, *Massacre at Sand Creek: How Methodists Were Involved in an American Tragedy* (Nashville: Abingdon Press, 2016).

and birth new life," such that "when we return to them, they challenge our compromises with the status quo, help us to remember what we should not forget, and inspire recommitment to who we ought to be."[31]

The originating power of gospel rested upon the active remembering—the spiritual anamnesis—of their authors and redactors.[32] The same power is required of Christian faith communities today, when we recall that the communal enterprise of teaching and learning is mediated by resurgent, insurgent memory work. It is an active remembering that resurrects lives stripped of sacred vitality, of essential aliveness. It is also an active remembering that holds us continuously accountable to ethical living that is congruent with the witnesses of gospel—good news to the poor, the captive, the oppressed. "Take, eat, this is my body, *which is now yours.* Remember me" (see also 1 Cor 11:23-26). These are words of a dangerous memory that instruct us about the Christian commitment to ensuring that no bodies are to be broken or blood shed because of our own action or inaction.

The question remains, in what ways is the church mired in organized forgetting?

The Bible as a Weapon of Mass Destruction

Just as the Christian church in North America is frequently forgetful about its history of domestic subjugation of peoples, it is also neglectful of the longer history and continuing status of colonizing encroachments across the globe. Key to implementing this latter form of violence was and is none other than the Bible. Today's average laity may be bored or bothered by irrelevant biblical teachings, and denominational agencies may scramble to produce materials that promote more lively "Bible-to-life" applications. In these efforts, good liberal Christians are quick to acknowledge that the Bible is too easily taken out of its historical contexts in order to rationalize unjust personal and social ideological biases, particularly to

31. Thomas H. Groome, *Educating for Life: A Spiritual Vision for Every Teacher and Parent* (Allen, TX: T. More, 1998), 359.

32. For a discussion on "spiritual anamnesis," see Peter Stuhlmacher, "Spiritual Remembering: John 14.26," in *The Holy Spirit and Christian Origins: Essays in Honor of James D.G. Dunn,* ed. Graham Stanton et al. (Grand Rapids: W. B. Eerdmans, 2004).

justify oppressive "isms"—a partial list includes racism, ethnocentrism, sexism, classism, colonialism, imperialism, heterosexism, jingoism, nativism, ableism, colorism. Raise the stakes a few notches, and we find ourselves reckoning not just with a misappropriated Bible, but a textual implement of massive and destructive social, cultural, and colonial power.

Biblical scholarship has provided us with ample evidence and analysis of using scripture for destructive ends. Traditions of emancipatory readings of the Bible have yielded strategies for reading against the grain of oppressive texts, and for reading with the "flesh-and-blood reader" to confront oppressively utilized texts—feminist, liberationist, indigenous, contextual, racial/ethnic cross-textual story-linking, queer reading,[33] to name a few.[34] Here I draw attention to a classic example that does not leave good liberal Christians off the hook when it comes to owning complicity in what has been called *scriptural violence.*

"Scriptural imperialism" is the historically progressive vision of White European expansion, advanced not only with swords and treaties but also with the Bible (and "a case of gin").[35] In several field-rattling volumes, the prodigious scholar of the history of biblical interpretation R. S. Sugirtharajah makes this case concerning the impact of the Christian Bible

33. In an interesting study, Heather White argues that it was Protestant liberals who may have unwittingly introduced a "homosexualized" Bible to the wider public, with their zeal for the modernization of biblical translation, coupled with enduring adherence to biblicism (upholding the authority of the Bible) and eager embrace of the therapeutic sciences (psychiatry and psychology) to interpret human sexuality. See Heather Rachelle White, *Reforming Sodom: Protestants and the Rise of Gay Rights* (Chapel Hill: University of North Carolina Press, 2015).

34. See, for instance, Mary F. Foskett and Jeffrey K. Kuan, *Ways of Being, Ways of Reading: Asian American Biblical Interpretation* (St. Louis: Chalice Press, 2006); Letty M. Russell, *Feminist Interpretation of the Bible* (Philadelphia: Westminster Press, 1985); Elisabeth Schüssler Fiorenza, *Wisdom Ways: Introducing Feminist Biblical Interpretation* (Maryknoll: Orbis Books, 2001); Fernando F. Segovia and Mary Ann Tolbert, *Reading from This Place,* vol. 2 (Minneapolis: Fortress Press, 1995); Vincent L. Wimbush and Rosamond C. Rodman, *African Americans and the Bible: Sacred Texts and Social Textures* (New York: Continuum, 2000); Devadasan Nithya Premnath and R. S. Sugirtharajah, *Border Crossings: Cross-Cultural Hermeneutics* (Maryknoll: Orbis Books, 2007); Kathleen O'Brien Wicker, Althea Spencer Miller, and Musa W. Dube Shomanah, *Feminist New Testament Studies: Global and Future Perspectives, Religion/Culture/Critique* (New York: Palgrave Macmillan, 2005).

35. R. S. Sugirtharajah, *The Bible and the Third World: Precolonial, Colonial, and Postcolonial Encounters* (Cambridge: Cambridge University Press, 2001), 45.

upon the two-thirds world: the Bible became weaponized in tandem with "European territorial colonization" of Asia, Africa, Latin America, and the Pacific.[36] The irony is that this had not always been the case. For instance, according to Sugirtharajah, encounters between (Nestorian) Christianity and Asia in pre-colonial times were subtle in impact and irenic in purpose. The harmonious—and some may dismiss pejoratively as syncretistic—co-existence of religions and sacred texts in premodern conditions seems inconceivable to modern imagination:

> The Bible did not arrive with the conquering army of a superior civilization in order to subjugate a weak and barbarous people but came with those on the fringes of society to parts of the world where civilization was thriving. The early harbingers of the good news were a motley crowd of missionaries, merchants, persecuted Christians, and travelers with hardly any political power or ambition to conquer.[37]

That changed with modern progressivism, when "the introduction of the Bible and Christian faith to foreign lands was used to justify the political and military aggression of the West."[38] Theologically, preoccupation shifted from Pauline exhortations of peaceful comingling of cultures and faiths to the Matthean commission: "Therefore, go . . ." (Matt 28:19).[39] Interestingly, the command of this familiar Great Commission is to "*teach* all nations" (translated most explicitly as "teaching" in the King James Version, the "'national Bible' of the English people"[40]). This verse continues to galvanize many Christians and their denominations today. Yet how often do we pause to consider that the call to the earth-wide spread of "good news" was a "call-to-arms" in ways more lethal than missional? Seen like this, the narrative arc of Luke-Acts takes on more ominous mean-

36. Ibid.

37. R. S. Sugirtharajah, *The Bible and Asia: From the Pre-Christian Era to the Postcolonial Age* (Cambridge: Harvard University Press, 2013), 3.

38. Pui-lan Kwok, *Postcolonial Imagination and Feminist Theology* (Louisville, KY: Westminister John Knox, 2005), 61.

39. R. S. Sugirtharajah, ed. *The Postcolonial Bible* (Sheffield: Sheffield Academic Press, 1998), 95.

40. Sugirtharajah, *The Bible and Asia*, 4.

ing. We see an internalized logic that justifies outward movements: we are transmitting—through deliberate modes of Christian institution—our good news to the world, and we do so under divine mandate.

Invigorated by renewed focus on this Great Commission, ecclesial infrastructures sprang up alongside colonial establishments: such agencies as the British and Foreign Bible society, founded in 1804, committed to the dissemination of the printed Christian Bible at affordable prices to every hand around the globe.[41] The Protestant fervor drove the translation of scripture into local vernaculars. Embedded within this evangelical zeal, however, was disdain for indigenous beliefs and practices:

> Not only the heathen, but the speech of the heathen, must be Christianized. Their language itself needs to be born again. Their very words have to be converted from foul meanings and base uses and baptized into a Christian sense, before those words can convey the great truths and ideas of the Bible.[42]

Not only must the heathens be converted, so too must their own language, allegedly because "only the Bible is the book of the whole human race."[43] Forged by and in tandem with White colonial desires, such Protestant missionary fervor turned the Great Commission into a curriculum for what we will subsequently explore as a "banking" approach to biblical teaching:

> [This interpretation of the] Great Commission demands or encourages a passive, banking model of education that does not value dialogue. Certain people, historically white Christians, have been (and in some places and spaces still are) considered the primary and most competent teachers of all others; and many marginalized peoples have been so convinced, worshipping at the altar of white superiority and sacrificing their own agency of critical engagement, self-definition, and cultural identity. Dialogue is

41. Sugirtharajah, *The Bible and the Third World*, 46–60.

42. The Bible Society Report, *The Book above Every Book* (London: The Bible House, 1910), 22; cited in Sugirtharajah, *The Bible and the Third World*, 59.

43. The Bible Society Report, 30–31.

deterred and proscribed by persons who consider themselves "the owners of truth and knowledge, for whom all non-members" are other.[44]

What I am presenting here is not new or original. Most serious students of biblical interpretation ought to know this by now. We also know from postcolonial scholarship that colonial encounters are multidirectional, not unilateral. Colonized subjects are creative tricksters when navigating in the shadow of empire—some resist colonizing biblicism, some use the Bible to protest against imperial power, some engage in their own subversive interpretation of the Bible.[45] What I highlight here is the fact that it was *educative* endeavors that facilitated the enterprise of colonial expansion so well. As practical theologians such as HyeRan Kim-Cragg and Swee Hong Lim have argued, the colonial curriculum made masterful use of "story and song"—texts of the Christian Bible, and the tunes of Christian worship—as pedagogic implements of cultural suppression and/or erasure, albeit not without resistance. The exportation of Bible-based curricula or liturgical and musical expressions from the West to the global south often facilitated the annulment of local, indigenous cultures and traditions.[46] The widespread Christian song "I Have Decided to Follow Jesus" expresses such embraced curricular agenda: there is "no turning back" to former cultural-religious practices or expressions.[47]

To this day, the supremacy of White colonial (re)presentation of biblical truth and knowledge pervades. Open a random catalog of main-

44. Paulo Freire, *Pedagogy of the Oppressed* (New York: Herder and Herder, 1970), 71; cited in Smith, "US Colonial Missions to African Slaves," 3.

45. See Sugirtharajah, *The Bible and Asia*, chapters 3-4. Additionally, not every agent of colonial power submitted uncritically to imperial agenda. See, for instance, Sugirtharajah's discussion of the hermeneutical "dissent" of Bishop John William Colenso (1814–83), who served in Natal, South Africa, and became a staunch critic of the British colonial empire. Sugirtharajah, *The Bible and the Third World*, chap. 3.

46. HyeRan Kim-Cragg, *Story and Song: A Postcolonial Interplay between Christian Education and Worship*, American University Studies Series VII, Theology and Religion (New York: Peter Lang, 2012); Swee Hong Lim, "Sacred Song for All God's Children: A Perspective on Post-Colonial Asian Congregational Song," in *Complex Identities in a Shifting World: Practical Theological Perspectives,* ed. Robert Mager, Pamela Couture, Pamela McCarroll, and Natalie Wigg-Stevenson (Zurich: Lit Verlag GmbH & Co. KG Wien, 2015).

47. Lim, "Sacred Song for All God's Children," 139–40.

stream church educational resources, and we find evidence of the implicit curricula of a middle-classed whitestream—from visual aesthetics (e.g., White-appearing Jesus, Mary, and Joseph) to curricular content (e.g., topical studies that correspond more with the personal, spiritual, or social angst of majority culture).[48] If our Bible studies continue to be no more than a retrieval of golden nuggets of biblical truth for sanitized contemporary living, if we deliberately continue to organize the forgetting of historical and contemporary scriptural violence, then biblical teachings will continue their trend of becoming increasingly irrelevant, as Foster declared long ago. Worse yet, in perpetuating uncritical use of the Bible, we are in effect sustaining the use of scripture as an enduring weapon of massive spiritual, psychic destruction.

The Church as Fractured Sanctuary: A Habitus of DisImagination

"It is no secret that the LGBT community is often marginalized or ostracized by Christian churches who hold the view that such 'lifestyles' are considered contrary to the teaching of the Bible," writes Barry C., a United Church of Christ hospital chaplain.[49] A quick poll among local clergy reveals the painful truths about the fragile, if not fractured, nature of Christian faith communities: ecumenical partnerships are stalled because one congregation in the community is "Open and Affirming"[50] to any and all persons regardless of sexual orientation; church folk reciting "bootstrap theology" to justify indifference to surrounding evidence of poverty and homeless; predominantly White, aging congregations frightened by the loss of identity yet shamed by inherited privilege. We can easily add to this list numerous other forms of power abuse shielded by ecclesial power, and acknowledge Foster's indictment of the church's captivity to cultural status quo.

48. In her book, HyeRan Kim-Cragg provides a helpful analysis of some enduring challenges found even in so-called progressive church curricular resources. According to Kim-Cragg, the materials may proffer more diverse and inclusive biblical viewpoints, yet they fall short in addressing the complexities and contradictions of the biblical canon, and do not go far enough in engaging strategies of biblical interpretation from global, postcolonial perspectives.

49. Barry C. is a pseudonym. Personal communication, July 2016.

50. The nomenclature of the United Church of Christ.

The question remains as to how faith communities as a collective, and persons of faith as individuals, could function against the grain of their presumably foundational ethic of peace, love, justice, righteousness, shalom. Are there vortices of *dis*imagination at work—parallel to Giroux's *dis*imagination machine as discussed in chapter 2—that have rewired our theological DNA, our *habitus*,[51] our internalized social conditioning, such that we have lost the capacity to imagine anything other than the dominant status quo in which we are mired?

Theologically speaking, a Christian faith community becomes a "sanctuary for injustice" rather than justice-seeking beloved community when it colludes with systems of corruption and exploitation, and contributes to the public legitimization of such reality. It is the systemic corruption of which Old Testament scholar Walter Brueggemann writes when comparing and contrasting the Solomonic "royal consciousness" with that of "prophetic imagination."[52] In this "royal consciousness," God is domesticated within the glorious architectures of human power. We expect God to belong on our side, and in the established spaces that we demarcate, rather than out there, in holy open places unsuspecting to us and uncontrollable by us. All four Gospels recount an enraged Jesus driving corrupt merchants and money-changers out of the temple. There lies a biblical example of outraged rejection of the human price tag placed on grace and reconciliation,[53] a "prophetic imagination" that sees deeply into the root of unjust laws and practices and demands a corrective of such internalized logic, or *habitus*, in the light of the kingdom—or better, kin-dom—of God.

Alarmingly, the theological "royal consciousness" reproduces itself by the lull of status quo, shape-shifting through time into such variations as Christian supersessionism, colonial Manifest Destiny, kyriarchy,[54]

51. See chapter 6 for further discussion of the concept of *habitus*.

52. Walter Brueggemann, *The Prophetic Imagination*, 2nd ed. (Minneapolis: Fortress Press, 2001).

53. See Marcus J. Borg and John Dominic Crossan, *The Last Week: The Day-by-Day Account of Jesus's Final Week in Jerusalem* (San Francisco: HarperSanFrancisco, 2006).

54. Coined by feminist biblical scholar Elizabeth Schüssler Fiorenza, *kyriarchy* refers to systems of intersecting, oppressive rule. See Schüssler Fiorenza, *Wisdom Ways*. The current political development within the United States suggests that we may very well be experiencing a form of *plutocracy*, the rule of the wealthy.

heteropatriarchy,[55] and racial supremacy. This harkens back to the case in the previous chapter concerning the theological logics of racism. Christian faith communities need to wrestle with the ways in which our very own theological toolkits, the elements of our theological worldview, are implicitly buttressing a "just world syndrome"[56] in which we are typically right, over against a world in need of our scale of justice. Michael Emerson and Christian Smith may have exposed the theological toolkits that scaffold White evangelical obliviousness to systemic racism in *Divided by Faith*, but research on liberal mainline churches shows not much better conditions. The mainline Protestant congregations profiled in the Pew Research Center's 2014 Religious Landscape Study are 86 percent White. Studies of intentional efforts toward interracial mixing yield that "diverse congregations do not ensure racial and ethnic harmony," and that congregations reporting multicultural diversity continue to exhibit patterns of White dominance.[57] Cultural captivity prevails unless we bring to light the enduring conditioning of *dis*imagination that organizes the life of faith communities. Thus, despite diminishing numeric shares,[58] mainline Protestantism still enjoys the safety net of societal and institutional values, habits, inheritances, and infrastructures. It is a daunting challenge for cognizant old-line denominations to reckon with the privilege of

55. *Heteropatriarchy* refers to the intertwining of patriarchal and heterosexist norms and value assumptions that privilege the systemic advantage and dominance of the social categories straight, White, men. See these brief but helpful introductions: Andrea Smith, "Dismantling Hierarchy, Queering Society," *Tikkun* 25, no. 4 (2010); Traci C. West, "Visions of Womanhood: Beyond Idolizing Heteropatriarchy," *Union Seminary Quarterly Review* 58, nos. 3–4 (2004).

56. James Waller, *Becoming Evil: How Ordinary People Commit Genocide and Mass Killing* (Oxford: Oxford University Press, 2002).

57. Putnam and Campbell, *American Grace*, 318; Korie L. Edwards, *The Elusive Dream: The Power of Race in Interracial Churches* (Oxford: Oxford University Press, 2008).

58. The Pew Research Center's widely accessed statistical reports confirm a decline of the "Christian share of the population"—from 78.4% in 2007 to 70.6% in 2014. Non-Christian faiths—comprised of Jewish, Muslim, Buddhist, Hindu, other faiths and world religions—see a rise from 4.7 percent to 5.9 percent, while self-reported "Unaffiliated" numbers see a 6.7 percent increase from 16.1 percent to 22.8 percent. See the Pew Research Center's 2014 Religious Landscape Study, accessed July 29, 2016, www.pewforum.org/religious-landscape-study/racial-and-ethnic-composition/.

historic, systemic, and cumulative advantage, while wrestling with escalating uncertainties about the future of their identity, unity, and purpose.

A different dimension to the vulnerability of faith communities relates to the issue of "spatial justice."[59] It is a spatial fragility configured by a conjuncture of broader societal *dis*imagination discussed in the previous chapter. Congregations split over space, and they wrestle with how to vitalize decrepit facilities; but congregations—especially non-Christian gatherings—must also fight for the right to exist in public space. The controversy over the Park 51 (Cordoba House) Initiative in New York City is now a classic case-in-point to illustrate the geopolitics of sacred space. What was proposed to be an Islamic Community Center in Lower Manhattan is vehemently condemned with public vitriol as a "Ground Zero Mosque" that supposedly dishonors the memory of victims of the terror attack on September 11, 2001.[60] There is also the reality of spatial violence when houses of worship become the target and the site of hate crimes. It is suggested that "most religiously motivated hate crimes are directed against property,"[61] but historical and current events remind us that in addition to churches being burned down, innocent lives can be extinguished during an ordinary evening Bible study by hate-based violence, as was the case in Charleston, South Carolina.[62]

Given such fragile and volatile milieu, how do the catechetical cultures of the church correspond faithfully to the complex events of the world, beyond quick technical fixes?[63] In the immediate aftermath of Sep-

---

59. Charles Lloyd Cohen, *Gods in America: Religious Pluralism in the United States* (New York: Oxford University Press, 2013), 64.

60. Ibid.

61. Ibid., 59.

62. Lindsey Bever, "Five Predominantly Black Southern Churches Burn within a Week: Arson Suspected in at Least Three" *The Washington Post*, June 29, 2015, www.washingtonpost.com/news/morning-mix/wp/2015/06/29/six-predominately-black-southern-churches-burn-within-a-week-with-arson-suspected-in-at-least-three/; Roberta Costa et al., "Church Shooting Suspect Dylann Roof Captured amid Hate Crime Investigation," *The Washington Post*, June 18, 2015, https://www.washingtonpost.com/news/morning-mix/wp/2015/06/17/white-gunman-sought-in-shooting-at-historic-charleston-african-ame-church/?utm_term=.05ed6252e141.

63. Foster appealed for adaptive "event-full" education—faith exploration that engage both the rhythmic seasonal and occasional activities in the life of the church, and also unexpected irruptions of joy or tragedy. Foster, *Educating Congregations*, 43–47.

tember 11, philosophers of education took stock of an emerging cultural environment signified by some as an "age of terror": a resurgence of Pax Americana and Fortress West (evidenced by the affinity for walls and borders in the name of security); rising authoritarian backlash, globalization, and pragmatism; politically stoked clash of civilizations, with widening gaps between the global north and south; closed minds and closed society in the face of uncertainty and fear; civic engagement stunted by consumer culture.[64] More than a decade later, despite a surge of freedom movements led by youthful activism, religious voices strain to sustain prophetic notes amid an increasingly turbulent socio-cultural-political climate. What Charles Foster identified years ago rings true even more today: that the collapse of catechetical cultures that help to bridge faith and public life seems to be headed down an irreversible path.

Banking Curriculum

Educators know that education is a *political* endeavor. As Catholic educator Thomas Groome famously declared in his field-defining book *Christian Religious Education*, "Educational activity with pilgrims in time is a political activity. I understand political activity to be any deliberate and structured intervention in people's lives which attempts to influence how they live their lives in society."[65] What is emphasized first is an intentionality, deliberateness, structured, or disciplined ways by which we engage in the educational task. But more than that, following the philosophical assumption of Brazilian education reformer Paulo Freire, education is political because it is necessarily an intervention in people's lives, a relational interaction that reorganizes others' ways of being in the world for better or for worse.[66] Theologically speaking, education facilitates *conversion*—not in the confessional mode of pledging allegiance to

64. Elemer Hankiss, "Paideia in an Age of Uncertainty," in *Educating for Democracy: Paideia in an Age of Uncertainty*, ed. Alan M. Olson, David M. Steiner, and Irina S. Tuuli (Lanham, MD: Rowman & Littlefield, 2004).

65. Thomas H. Groome, *Christian Religious Education: Sharing Our Story and Vision* (San Francisco, CA: HarperSanFrancisco, 1980), 15.

66. See Paulo Freire, "Letter to North-American Teachers," in *Freire for the Classroom: A Sourcebook for Liberatory Teaching*, ed. Ira Shor (Portsmouth: Boynton/Cook, 1987), 212.

Jesus and the church, but rather in the sense of *turning* and a *tuning* of our heart, mind, body, and will toward transformative realities and commitments.[67] For this reason, practical theologian Mary Elizabeth Mullino Moore calls teaching a sacramental act—it is an activity in which ordinary means mediate the holy.[68]

Despite such higher ideals, public and religious educators agonize under the oppressive regimes of "banking" approaches to education. In his landmark book *Pedagogy of the Oppressed*, Paulo Freire spells out what he considers to be the pedagogic attitudes and practices characteristic of banking approaches to teaching.[69] Under this regime, learners are passive recipients of information, bestowed upon them by authoritarian teachers who are the fount of all knowledge. The teacher as subject deposits knowledge; the learner as object receives, banks, and regurgitates it. There is no place for curiosity and critical consciousness, which are requisite to a Freirean paradigm of discovery learning: "The capability of banking education to minimize or annul the student's creative power and to stimulate their credulity serves the interests of the oppressor, who care neither to have the world revealed nor to see it transformed."[70] Ultimately, educational banking characterizes colonizing pedagogies, for their interest is in "changing the consciousness of the oppressed, not the situation which oppresses them."[71] Concerns over marketable curriculum, entertaining lesson plans, and easy-to-use teacher's guides miss the mark if it they do not address the fundamental stuckness of educational paradigms that tame and even constrict theological imagination.[72]

---

67. Cf. HyeRan Kim-Cragg and Mai-Anh Le Tran, "Turning to the Other: Interdenominational, Interethnic, Interreligious Activism and a New Ecclesia," in Mager et al., *Complex Identities in a Shifting World.*

68. Mary Elizabeth Moore, *Teaching as a Sacramental Act* (Cleveland: Pilgrim Press, 2004).

69. Paulo Freire, *Pedagogy of the Oppressed*, trans. Myra Bergman Ramos, new rev. 20th-anniversary ed. (New York: Continuum, 1997), 52.

70. Ibid., 54.

71. Simone de Beauvoir, *La Pensee De Droite, Aujord'jui; St, El Pensamiento Politico De La Derecha* (Buenos Aires: 1963); cited in ibid., 55.

72. For helpful suggestions for how to evaluate theological curriculum, see Norma Cook Everist, *The Church as Learning Community: A Comprehensive Guide to Christian Education* (Nashville: Abingdon Press, 2002).

Good liberal Christians should also take note of a more pernicious practice of which they may be guilty: the exercise of "repressive tolerance."[73] A pedagogic version of the racial colorblind project, repressive tolerance celebrates a false sense of diversity; it assumes that learners can be presented with a number of ideas, values, traditions, then pick and choose what they want to embrace. It is a form of liberal, open-market approach educational planning: let the people have a choice in what they want to know, to learn, to do. What educators forget is that ideas come with deep social ideological conditioning. When a minoritized perspective is juxtaposed with a mainstream idea, the radical nature of the alternative is easily diluted and considered supplemental to the dominant norm. Consider the prevailing backlash to depictions of Jesus in any hue other than White. Consider why many readers of the Bible, when introduced to a plethora of equally valid approaches to biblical interpretation, would revert back to strategies with which they are more familiar (for conservative Christians, that may be biblicism; for liberals, it may be historical criticism). The power (and toxicity) of a dominant idea or practice is that it enjoys centrality within the status quo, and therefore does not easily give way to alternative options, which are often stereotypically caricatured as contextual or perspectival options (e.g., a "feminist" reading of the Bible is only for women, a "postcolonial" reading of the Bible is only for the subaltern). In the end, this approach to tolerance may appear all-inclusive, but when it fails to critique the ideological conditioning that sustains the prevailing dominant idea or practice, it runs the risk of further ostracizing alternatives that are marginal to the repressive norm.

Consider this pedagogic dilemma in the greater scheme of challenging oppressive theological ideas, and we see how curricular agendas that bank on either banking teaching or repressive tolerance are equally lethal to critical consciousness—characterized by the capacity for historical memory, critical thinking, self-reflexive dialogue, empathic courage, and ethopolitical agency to engage as an active disciple-citizen in the world.[74]

73. Stephen Brookfield and John D. Holst, *Radicalizing Learning: Adult Education for a Just World*, The Jossey-Bass Higher and Adult Education Series (San Francisco, CA: John Wiley, 2011), 190–97.

74. Giroux, *The Violence of Organized Forgetting*, 60–83.

Reset the Heart

To riff on a saying attributed to the Hindu mystic and guru Sri Ramakrishna, "Religious education is like a cow. It kicks but it gives milk, too."[75] Let me explain, in the language of two giants in the field.

Education, in its most fundamental sense, is "the reshaping of life's forms with end and without end," says Gabriel Moran in his book *Living Nonviolently*.[76] Religious education, following Moran-speak, has purpose, but no ending; it encompasses a multiplicity of forms by which we nourish and rear one another in what must be a "lifelong and lifewide"[77] commitment to active peaceful, nonviolent living. Now, the *telos* set forth by Moran and others like him is what religious educators "set our hearts" upon, following Sara Little's refresher on the root meaning of *credo* in her field-defining book *To Set One's Heart*. "Conscious attention to belief formation" is paramount for the teaching ministry of Christian faith communities, Little wrote, "to link lives of individuals and communities to larger, ultimate realities and purposes."[78] Linking purposeful teaching to the formation of holistic belief systems—not dogma, but meaning-making structures that connect mind (cognition), heart (affect), will (volition), and action (behavior)—Little provided us with this classic thesis: "Beliefs which engage the thinking powers of the person as they emerge out of and inform faith, sustained, reformed, and embodied by the faith community, can be an important factor in bringing *integration* and *integrity* to life."[79] To "believe," therefore, is not simply a matter of thinking or feeling one's way toward some set of truth. More profoundly, it is a setting of our hearts, a staking of ourselves and our life habits upon communally framed convictions that give meaning and pattern to how we live. Reli-

75. "Religion is like a cow. It kicks but gives milk, too." Jan Love, "Preface," in *Violence and Christian Spirituality: An Ecumenical Conversation*, ed. Emmanuel Clapsis (Brookline: Holy Cross Orthodox Press, 2007), xii.

76. Gabriel Moran, *Living Nonviolently: Language for Resisting Violence* (Lanham, MD: Lexington Books, 2011), 167.

77. Ibid., 164.

78. Sara Little, *To Set One's Heart: Belief and Teaching in the Church* (Atlanta: John Knox Press, 1983), 32, 21.

79. Ibid., 9. Emphasis in original.

gious education, then, is "intentional teaching" toward the chief aim of facilitating this emergence of "integration and integrity" between what we believe and how we live. It is the aim of giving milk for the flourishing of individuals, communities, and planetary life.

And yet, against such superb axiological assumptions, religious education also *kicks*—whether out of sheer muscular reflex or menacing premeditation. As suggested in this chapter, the educational enterprises of our respective religious traditions have perplexingly served as implements[80] of terrorizing forces, both aggressive and passive.

Cognizance of this reality does not render us nihilistic, however. We have been taught by the wisdom of those who came before that Christian religious education is a communal enterprise of "drawing out"; the "artistic work" of creating, re-creating, fashioning, and refashioning communal life of faith for people "pledging their troth" to one another in covenants of love.[81] It is steady and disciplined reflection on matters of faith and formation; on visions of ultimate environment that sustain meaning and purpose for individuals and communities; on "deep, rich, complex, nuanced" languages of spiritual yearnings that "regulate and shape"[82] our lives, lest "bread alone kills us."[83] It requires cultivation of vital ecologies of learning that stand in contrast to the surrounding death worlds, environments fertile for deliberate and continuous action and reflection upon what it means to be *Christian*, to be *religious* and *spiritual*, to be faithful and transformational in community, in daily life, and in the world.

More systematically, the ministry of education in the church entails concerted engagement with individual and communal sources of meaning: life stories, collective histories, lived experiences of faith, practical wisdom

80. Hannah Arendt, *On Violence* (New York: Harcourt, 1970), 2.

81. Maria Harris, *Fashion Me a People: Curriculum in the Church* (Louisville, KY: Westminster/John Knox Press, 1989), 40–41. Parker J. Palmer, *To Know as We Are Known: Education as a Spiritual Journey* (San Francisco: HarperSanFrancisco, 1993), 43.

82. Craig R. Dykstra, *Growing in the Life of Faith: Education and Christian Practices* (Louisville, KY: Geneva Press, 1999), 7.

83. Dorothee Soelle, *Death by Bread Alone: Texts and Reflections on Religious Experience* (Philadelphia, PA: Fortress Press, 1978), 3–4.

on strategies for livelihood.[84] Simultaneously, there is critical study of the reservoirs of tradition that guide communal action and reflection: the repertoires of religious stories, signs, symbols, rituals, their meanings and interpretations; and how they are culturally, historically, politically, and symbolically reincarnated in new ways in the life of individuals and communities. Moreover, Christian religious education explores and facilitates the process of *traditioning*—echoing, *katecheo*—within communities, attending to how dynamic religious repertoires provide raw materials as well as contestable templates for meaning *made* and *lived* from one generation to the next. In this, religious teaching and learning make "accessible and manifest"[85] resources that help to raise consciousness about how a community appropriates traditions, how it is formed by them, and how it transforms them. The driving *telos* of such high-spirited work is to equip persons and communities to "face into the world" as creative, generative public theologians compelled by a world in need of repair.[86] Through the ministry of education, communities learn and practice how to incarnate on earth the abounding grace, love, and hope of God's peaceable realm. It is a vision of a *Pax Globalis* or *Pax Universalis*[87] arising out of a mindfulness of our place the *oikumenê*, "the inhabited world," and out of deep attunement to the other in whom we are existentially and spiritually interdependent.[88]

Interlude

As stated, a stark analysis of educational flaws and losses does not petrify us toward inaction, nor does it excuse the forces of institutional

84. See Jack Mezirow, *Learning as Transformation: Critical Perspectives on a Theory in Progress*, The Jossey-Bass Higher and Adult Education Series (San Francisco: Jossey-Bass, 2000).

85. Mary C. Boys, *Educating in Faith: Maps and Visions* (San Francisco: Harper & Row, 1989), 193.

86. Jack L. Seymour, ed. *Mapping Christian Education: Approaches to Congregational Learning* (Nashville: Abingdon Press, 1997), 121.

87. Elemer Hankiss, "*Paideia* in an Age of Uncertainty," in *Educating for Democracy: Paideia in an Age of Uncertainty*, ed. Alan M. Olson, David M. Steiner, and Irina S. Tuuli (Lanham, MD: Rowman & Littlefield Publishers, 2004), 152.

88. Mary C. Boys and Sara S. Lee, *Christians & Jews in Dialogue: Learning in the Presence of the Other* (Woodstock: SkyLight Paths Pub., 2006).

inertia. We know that there are faithful individuals and congregations engaged in valiant action against the public pedagogies of *dis*imagination. We know that there are communities of faith innovating their way against educational malpractice. With the above vision for lifelong and lifewide religious teaching and learning, we turn attention toward discovery of how Christian faith communities may look to one another for clues on how to actualize the possibilities of resurrectional, insurrectional hope in the midst of violence's *dis*imagination. We turn to ask, what (re)new(ed) practices of faith and educational leadership can help us to unlearn violence and relearn hope?

For this exploration, I solicited the participation of fourteen[89] local ministers to participate as theological reflectors. They read a precis of this book and of each chapter, and offered responses in writing to specific reflection questions that I posed. I asked each to reflect on the questions in light of their own ministerial context, and to share vignettes or anecdotes that might illuminate the themes explored in the second half of the book, as though they were "riffing" with me on ideas concerning ministry and public witness. In the end, their contributions are woven into the following three chapters, as I explore the challenges and possibilities of *communicable* love, *redeemable* faith, and *educable* hope.

89. I extended the invitation to twenty-two individuals whom I had known from previous ministry and seminary connections. Of the fourteen who could participate, twelve are Christians of various mainline denominations, two are Unitarians active in congregational ministry. All fourteen were seminary trained and serving in congregational settings, either as ordained, licensed, or paid ministerial staff. These "theological reflectors" contributed their written reflections in three rounds over a month-long period. At the end, some of us who were local to St. Louis gathered in my home for a meal to debrief the experience. The lively conversation demonstrated these leaders' ability to amplify the themes of this book and connect them to their ministerial realities.

Chapter 4

Practicing Communicability

On September 30, 2014, Liberian national Thomas Eric Duncan became the first patient diagnosed with the Ebola virus in the United States. He died at Texas Health Presbyterian Hospital in Dallas, Texas, nine days later.[1] Breaking the news cycles just less than two months after the shooting death of Michael Brown in Ferguson on August 9, Mr. Duncan became a different yet familiar reminder of how lives—Black lives in particular—meet their demise under entwining systems of "infectious diseases," in which they are ironically configured as threatening pollutants. In microbiological terms, Thomas Duncan was the carrier who brought the Ebola virus into the United States, thereby infecting two nurses from within this country's borders, before his death on October 8. However, Mr. Duncan also died a social death when a virus of fear in the public imagination turned him into a foreign contagion that invaded the borders, safety, security, and well-being of what is supposed to be an impenetrable nation.[2] Amid concerns on the part of family and friends that Mr. Duncan may not have received proper and timely treatment due to his race, Liberian government officials were quick to distance themselves by publicly chastising

1. Norimitsu Onishi, "U.S. Patient Aided Pregnant Liberian, Then Took Ill," *The New York Times*, October 1, 2014, www.nytimes.com/2014/10/02/world/africa/ebola-victim-texas-thomas-eric-duncan.html?_r=0.

2. Manny Fernandez and Dave Philipps, "Death of Thomas Eric Duncan in Dallas Fuels Alarm over Ebola," *The New York Times*, October 8, 2014, www.nytimes.com/2014/10/09/us/ebola-us-thomas-eric-duncan.html.

him for his alleged "unpardonable" non-disclosure upon arrival in the United States of known contact with the infectious disease.[3]

The same virus of fear also struck down the marked body of Michael Brown—in his case, posthumously, in vitriolic public debates about his character and justifications of his death.[4] Daily, even before any legal or moral guilt is established, the court of public opinion, abetted by procedural obfuscations, is quick to find a victim to blame and shame. It should not be necessary to argue whether or not the victim is an innocent scapegoat,[5] nor is it the focal point of analysis here. What comes to light in the social deaths of the Michael Browns and Thomas Duncans is the sinister virus of fear. Dormant yet also chronic in public imagination, it is activated through violent outbreaks, striking ruthlessly a host of otherly marked bodies: racialized bodies, sexualized bodies, the transient bodies of those homeless, LGBTQ bodies, the "alien" bodies of undocumented immigrants. A fear-stricken social imagination deems them dangerous upon contact: we must not let them near, we must quarantine them, we must disinfect ourselves of them, they will hurt us or deplete our systems. If they touch us, we will die.

"Communicable diseases" (the original first two words for the acronym CDC) have biological and moral dimensions. The spread of disease exposes human ignorance, vulnerability, and promiscuity: we unknowingly facilitate its spread, our immune systems are too vulnerable to have fought against it, or we defiantly transgress barriers that safeguard protection.[6] Human carriers easily become scapegoats: they are "examples of the

3. Jacque Wilson, Catherine E. Shoichet, and Holly Yan, "Ebola Patient's Leaving Liberia Was 'Unpardonable,' Its President Says" *CNN*, October 3, 2014, www.cnn.com/2014/10/02/health/ebola-us/index.html.

4. Six days after his shooting, the Ferguson Police Department released a video recording of Michael Brown grabbing a box of cigarillos from a local convenient store and engaging in a tussle with the store clerk. The video release, as well as the ensuing grand jury process and decision to not indict police officer Darren Wilson, was condemned by supporters and activists as evidence of character assassination and judicial bias. Tanzina Vega, Timothy Williams, and Erik Eckholm, "Emotions Flare in Missouri amid Police Statements," *The New York Times*, August 15, 2014, www.nytimes.com/2014/08/16/us/darren-wilson-identified-as-officer-in-fatal-shooting-in-ferguson-missouri.html?smid=pl-share.

5. The forceful theory of scapegoat and mimetic violence was proffered by the renowned René Girard. See *Violence and the Sacred* (Baltimore: Johns Hopkins University Press, 1977).

6. This is not to suggest that public concerns about infectious diseases are all indicative

transgressions of the group for which they symbolically suffered."[7] Epidemics justify "regulation with 'terrifying urgency,'" and they set in motion "'the administrative machinery for disease prevention, sanitary super-vision, and, in general, protection of community health.'"[8] Quarantine and surveillance become two crucial strategies for containment of disease—and in the age of transnationalism, global surveillance is justified not only for reasons of national defense, but also as a matter of "national public health."[9] An infection/infestation is an invasion of the body—physical and national.

The enduring struggle with communicability characterizes the complicated nature of human community. Epidemiology—the study of communicable diseases—provides a unique way to wade through this quagmire. Community requires human contact, and we live in a world in which community is configured by communicability, or the capability of impactful transference through contact.[10] *Communicability* is that capacity which defines the social nature of human existence.

What if we were to assess the Christian faith community in terms of its communicable capacity?

Community Configured by Communicability

In her fascinating book *Contagious*,[11] professor of English Priscilla Wald breaks down the scripts of outbreak narratives in scientific and

of mass hysteria. In recent news, the problem of pervasive transmission of HIV/AIDS through abusive misogynistic practices against women and girls was again brought to light with incidents such as the arrest of an HIV-infected man in Malawi who claim to be a hired "hyena" whose function is to have sex with girls for ritualistic purposes; Travis M. Andrews, "Malawi Police Arrest HIV-Positive Man Paid by Parents to Have Sex with Scores of Young Girls," *The Washington Post*, July 27, 2016, www.washingtonpost.com/news/morning-mix/wp/2016/07/27/malawi-police-arrest-hiv-positive-man-paid-by-parents-to-have-sex-with-scores-of-young-girls/.

7. Priscilla Wald, *Contagious: Cultures, Carriers, and the Outbreak Narrative* (Durham, NC: Duke University Press, 2008), 17.

8. Ibid.

9. Ibid., 25.

10. Ibid., 12.

11. Ibid.

popular literature since the discovery of the first known "chronic typhoid germ distributor" in 1907—the first human carrier, popularly known as "Typhoid Mary." Analyzing depictions and discussions of Cold War epidemics, HIV/AIDS, the initial discovery of Ebola, to SARS, Wald sketches how "epidemiology dramatizes human beings' mortal struggle with their environment, social and biological."[12]

According to Wald, whether it is in our attempts to understand microbes or social relations, human beings are plagued by the Other as we grapple with the paradox: human intercourse binds us together, but it also makes us sick.[13] Contagion literally means "to touch together," and was first used in the fourteenth century to refer to the "circulation of ideas and attitudes," often with a connotation of social and moral "danger or corruption."[14] As industrialization facilitated urban constructions of community, "the growth of cities gave rise to what [was considered to be] 'promiscuous' social spaces: people literally and figuratively bumping up against each other in smaller spaces and larger numbers than ever before."[15] Like the fear of disease, the social fear of contagious ideas is palpable and visceral: "Both [display] the power and danger of bodies in contact and [demonstrate] the simultaneous fragility and tenacity of social bonds."[16]

Communicable Christian Community

Community is a hallmark of the Christian faith. It is a prized feature of numerous biblically based and theologically grounded approaches to Christian faith formation.[17] Even disenchanted, dis-establishment spiri-

12. Ibid., 21.

13. Ibid., 2.

14. Ibid., 12.

15. Ibid., 14.

16. Priscilla Wald, *Contagious: Cultures, Carriers, and the Outbreak Narrative*, a John Hope Franklin Center Book (Durham: Duke University Press, 2007), ebook edition, introduction.

17. For a survey of important articulation of approaches to education in communities of faith within the United States, see Jack L. Seymour, *Teaching the Way of Jesus: Educating Christians for Faithful Living* (Nashville: Abingdon Press, 2014), chap. 4.

tual seekers insist that the church is not a building, but rather a people bound by the fellowship of community.[18] The popular biblical standard-bearer for such idyllic vision of life in community is none other than the Lukan depiction in Acts 2:42-47: the early followers of the Jesus movement ate, prayed, and loved, and their numbers grew on a daily basis.

Indeed, a community of faith today is also configured by these very public curricula of eating, praying, and loving. The trouble is that, misguided by contemporary cultural assumptions of market-driven individualism, we tend to misunderstand these to be personal life habits of privatized fulfillment rather than messy communal acts of intimate, sacred nature. We assume idealistically that *eating* first and foremost belongs to the arena of home and hearth, in such well-stocked and compartmentalized settings as kitchens and dining rooms, until we factor in the economics of eating out, and the politics of the food, advertising, production, manufacturing, and service industries that make possible or impossible our abilities to eat—even to eat around dinner tables—on a daily basis. We assume that *loving* also is a personal thing—the arenas for which are largely hidden spaces, whether or not permissible (from the bedroom to public parks), until we factor in the public morality plays, and socio-cultural and legislative regulations of *how* and *whom* to love. We also assume that *praying* belongs to self-select private or sectarian domains, until we are reminded by liturgical theologians such as Marjorie Procter-Smith that praying is a very political act, and that sometimes death-dealing community can render us silent—unable and unwilling to pray.[19]

This public/private confusion presents a vexing irony for people of faith: we love the idea of community, we exhort one another to "build community," and yet we have a hard time figuring out why it is hard to be in community, and we struggle to admit that sometimes being in community *hurts*.

18. See, for instance, Diana Butler Bass, *Christianity after Religion: The End of Church and the Birth of a New Spiritual Awakening* (New York: HarperOne, 2012).

19. Marjorie Procter-Smith, *Praying with Our Eyes Open: Engendering Feminist Liturgical Prayer* (Nashville: Abingdon Press, 1995), 10.

The Breakdown of Communal Responsibility

Dorothy Bass, in a 1995 essay with religious educators Mary Boys and Sara Lee, presents one possible root of this problem: the breakdown of communal responsibility, traceable—ironically—to the Protestant tenet of the "priesthood of all believers." For Bass, the enduring conundrum for Protestant Christian education in the latter part of the twentieth century is this: "the conflation of the priesthood of all believers with secular or civil religious forms of individualism."[20] When it emerged as a burst of renewing energy in the Reformation era, the priesthood of all believers was a theological conviction that motivated lay Christians "to take seriously their own calling to study, to serve, and even to lead as members of the Body of Christ."[21] However, over the years, the social, cultural, and economic landscape of the United States reduced religion to a private, individual matter, and construed "life habits" as being nurtured and based on "consumerism and autonomy." Bass asserts,

> The Reformation heritage of individual freedom for ministry has become confused with American ideals of individual freedom from obligation. . . . Belonging and believing are seen as matters of personal choice, and it is difficult to sustain communities within which growth in faith can be nurtured.[22]

Life habits have been nurtured in such a way that we have confused "freedom for ministry" with "freedom from communal responsibility." Boyung Lee puts it bluntly in her book *Transforming Congregations through Community:* sometimes, what the church calls community is really only a "gathering of individuals in reciprocal relationships," who will opt out of the collective when things are no longer interesting, or when the demands of the group become too burdensome.[23]

---

20. Mary C. Boys, Sara S. Lee, and Dorothy C. Bass, "Protestant, Catholic, Jew: The Transformative Possibilities of Educating across Religious Boundaries," *Religious Education* 90, no. 2 (1995): 268. The second major issue for Bass is Protestantism's interfaith struggle and its inability to sustain public Christian identity outside of presumed cultural dominance.

21. Ibid.

22. Ibid., 268–69.

23. Boyung Lee, *Transforming Congregations through Community: Faith Formation from the Seminary to the Church* (Louisville, KY: Westminster John Knox Press, 2013), 14–15.

"Community of the Age of Salvation"

Against such *dis*imagination, many Christian faith communities have drawn on another biblical witness for renewed vision: the prayer that Jesus taught his disciples, and the way it offered a new imagination on how to pray, how to eat, and how to love. Crafted for a band of followers who already knew how to pray in private devotion and public worship, the Jesus prayer (Luke 11:2-4; Matt 6:9-13) was an Aramaic prayer, taught for vernacular tongues, the words and form of which echo the ancient Jewish prayer *Kaddish*.[24] As biblical scholars argue, the distinction lies in how each petition of the Jesus prayer leans into an "eschatology becoming actualized."[25] It is "a brief summary of the fundamentals of Jesus' proclamation" about the saving work that God has already begun.[26] Joachim Jeremias's exposition helps make this point: "Jesus' disciples recognized themselves as a community, or more exactly as the *community of the age of salvation*, and . . . they requested of Jesus a prayer which would bind them together and identify them, in that it would bring to expression their chief concern."[27]

Solidifying a vision for an alternative already-but-not-yet community, Jesus gave his disciples a prayer that expanded their imagination for communicability, or their capacity for earthly contact. The prayer Jesus taught de-privatized and de-individualized the urgent concerns of daily life ("*Our* Father, . . . Give *us* . . . Forgive *us as we* . . . Lead *us* not . . . but deliver *us*"), and made inseparable matters of earth and heaven, for in the realm of God, "earthly things [are] hallowed."[28] Thus, this "community of the age of salvation"—a community that actively realizes with God wholeness and fullness of all life—is one that has the capacity to imagine the following:

---

24. Joachim Jeremias, *The Prayers of Jesus*, Studies in Biblical Theology (Naperville, IL: A. R. Allenson, 1967), 76, 93, 98.

25. Ibid., 107.

26. Ibid., 77, 99, 107.

27. Ibid., 94. Italics added.

28. Ibid., 101.

That life can be abundant through daily practices of eating and drinking,
That the violence of vicious cycles of economic bondage would be interrupted,
That there would be deliverance from unjust trials and tribulations,
That we would learn to repent from our violent allergies to one another,
That human contact is sacred contact,
for God's kin(g)dom has come, and is still coming, and all earthly things are hallowed.

This paradigmatic prayer—paradigmatic in its capacity to frame a worldview and way of life for those who live by it—coheres with what the Gospel writers later remembered about the way of Jesus. Luke, for instance, imagined in Jesus a ministry of great reversals of the human social order: "Jesus' message heralds a new community, a new humanity. . . . [A] radically new type of community has been hailed by New Testament scholarship as the principal effect and even the primary intention of Jesus' proclamation of the kingdom of God."[29]

Of all the things this kin(g)dom,[30] *basileia*, is purported to be, at its center is divine interruption of human affairs, the range of which extends beyond the personal and spiritual to encompass social, economic, and political arenas. As proclaimed in the Gospel of Luke, the rule of God is about "boundary-transgressing, inside-out reversals."[31] It is a rule that subverts religiously sanctioned categories of "sinner" and "saved," challenges culturally demarcated us vs. them binaries, and declares dignity and worth in those whom society considers lowly.

How then do we as the church live in to this transgressive way of being with one another?

---

29. Thomas Wieser, "Community: Its Unity, Diversity and Universality," *Semeia* 33 (1985): 84.

30. Following feminist theological sensibility, I use the expression *kin(g)dom* instead of *kingdom* to counter and resist the heteropatriarchal imperialism latent in the symbolic meanings related to monarchy and top-down forms of power expressed by the latter.

31. John T. Carroll, "Luke, Gospel of," in *The Interpreter's Dictionary of the Bible*, vol. 3, ed. Katherine Doob Sakenfeld et al. (Nashville: Abingdon Press, 2008), 729.

Practicing Communicability: (In)decent Contact, Carnal Worship, Boundless Table

If the paradigm of Jesus guides the church's public curricula and practices of eating, praying, and loving, then how might we imagine the concrete praxis[32] of its communicable capacity? I suggest the following three: (In)decent Contact (loving); Carnal Worship (praying); and Boundless Table (eating). These three generative themes arose out of reflection on the events of that Moral Monday in October 2014 (narrated in chapter 1), when I witnessed gritty rain- and sweat-soaked contact among strangers who occupied the streets of Ferguson to enact public liturgies against injustice, and whose stamina was sustained when they partook together in "Eucharistic" meals of pizza, donuts, and coffee provided through the hospitality of yet other strangers. Surely these must be practices essential to Christian communicability.

I set out to solicit reflections from a group of fourteen clergy colleagues, most of whom had had direct and indirect involvement in faith-based activism in Ferguson, and who continue to strive toward transformative ministry in their current congregational contexts. Their reflections give words to the fleshly examples witnessed on the ground.

(In)decent Contact

A Christian faith community that follows the way of Jesus knows that it is bound by incarnational love, a love that requires skin-to-skin contact. The conundrum is that we have enshrouded the rule of love in a self-preserving, contagion-resisting web of decency—our way of regulating the limits of who may come into contact with us. The late Argentinian theologian Marcella Althaus-Reid took on the rules of decency in theological praxis in her highly provocative book *Indecent Theology*.[33] For critical

32. Recall from chapter 1 that *praxis* names the melding of theory and practice; it is the integration of reflective action and practice-based reflection. Praxis is a notable development for religious education, and its use by Brazilian educational reformer Paulo Freire is an important source of inspiration.

33. *Indecent Theology: Theological Perversions in Sex, Gender and Politics* (New York: Routledge, 2000).

liberationists like her, theology is necessarily political because it organizes our patterns of believing, behaving, and belonging.[34] Awareness of this requires our vigilant attention to how theological ideas and faith practices are regulated by terms of inclusion and exclusion, which betray our biases about decent communicability. Under such regulation, it should be no surprise that communities of faith find themselves becoming hostile "combat zones" rather than fertile "contact zones."[35]

Communities (like Ferguson) plagued by violence know too well the harm of dangerous contact—the deliberate violation of the sacred intimacies and vitality of community. At the same time, communities in dangerous combat zones—in geographic spaces ripped apart by the violence of war, poverty, abuse, crime—have firsthand knowledge of the power of *in*decent contact, or risky human relationships that defy boundaries dictated by repressive social norms. The work of the "violence interrupters" of the Chicago-based organization Cure Violence is a compelling example. The 2011 award-winning documentary *The Interrupters* follows the stories of three former powerful gang members who became trained interventionists in the streets of Chicago.[36] Seasoned with the practical wisdom of street life, these self-described "violence interrupters" deftly place their bodies in dangerous contact zones each time they enter a volatile situation to deescalate tension.

Recalling that the Christian curriculum[37] of loving does require the risk of dangerous and *in*decent contact, I wonder what it is about our

34. See Diana Butler Bass, *Christianity after Religion: The End of Church and the Birth of a New Spiritual Awakening* (New York: HarperOne, 2012).

35. See HyeRan Kim-Cragg and Mai-Anh Le Tran, "Turning to the Other: Interdenominational, Interethnic, Interreligious Activism and a New Ecclesia," in *Complex Identities in a Shifting World: Practical Theological Perspectives*, ed. Robert Mager, Pamela Couture, Pamela McCarroll, and Natalie Wigg-Stevenson (Zurich: Lit Verlag GmbH & Co. KG Wien, 2015).

36. *The Interrupters*, PBS Frontline, accessed August 3, 2016, www.pbs.org/wgbh/frontline/film/interrupters/; "Award Winning Documentary on Cure Violence," Cure Violence, accessed August 3, 2016, http://cureviolence.org/resources/the-interrupters/.

37. *Curriculum* is used here in the sense developed by Maria Harris. Beyond printed resources or teaching materials, it is "a course to be run," the totality of experiences and conditions that forms and transforms teaching and learning. See *Fashion Me a People: Curriculum in the Church* (Louisville, KY: Westminster/John Knox Press, 1989), chap. 3.

daily "life habits" and "catechetical cultures" (Foster's expression for the church's educational infrastructures, as discussed in chapter 3) that stops us from implementing such a curriculum. Pursuing this query, I posed the following question to my group of ministerial reflection partners:

How/Where have you seen faith communities wrestle with the power and risks of human contact?

Pastor Stella M.[38] writes of the fear of vulnerable exposure to the other:

> In the church I currently serve, I have seen an interesting split in the ways in which folks struggle with the power and risks of human contact. On one hand, when it comes to engaging in ministry beyond their immediate (geographically) communities with folks who are different from them racially and socioeconomically, the church wrestles little with power and risk in their literal and figurative contact with these other humans. Primarily, I think, because the church folks have the privilege of removing themselves physically from these communities, and removing themselves figuratively from the risk and vulnerability of admitting a common humanity by focusing instead on the difference of "the others." When speaking with those in their communities about faith or engaging in local mission, folks in this same church feel overwhelmed by the risk involved because those with whom they are in contact are the people they live with and who look and live (mostly) just like them, and who (often) have just as much power than they do relationally. Which means that they cannot simply remove themselves from physical contact or from the figurative risks that come with an acknowledged common humanity and having to exist in a prolonged state of vulnerability that occurs in the context of relationship.

Faith communities—like other social entities—have an affinity for "internally similar" grouping and for internally recognizable power balances and differentials.[39] As Pastor Stella M. attests, to risk acknowledging a

38. To protect the privacy of ministerial settings, I refer to all of the reflection partners by pseudonyms. When appropriate, I keep denominational identifiers, but try to make geographic references vague enough so that the specific congregations would not be identified so easily.

39. Michael O. Emerson and Christian Smith, *Divided by Faith: Evangelical Religion and the Problem of Race in America* (Oxford: Oxford University Press, 2000), 141–50. Pastor Stella's observation points to an interesting dynamic that stymies much of what is considered local evangelism or local mission. Evangelism is typically defined as Christian witness for the sake of

"common humanity" with dissimilar strangers outside of our socially and geographically drawn boundaries is to let go of the securities that such boundaries supposedly assure. This frightens church folk, especially if contact with the other entails admission of our lack of power. What if, with our defenses down, we end up "catching something" from such risky contact?

Bruce J., an associate pastor of a congregation near Ferguson, Missouri, reflects on this honest struggle to make first contact with the non-churched:

> I think back to conversations with a couple of congregation members where the struggle was in how to start a conversation with non-church members. Though these members were caring and did interact well with non-church folks, there was still anxiety/uncertainty about how to make that initial contact. In some ways it seemed to be a fear of being rejected, saying the wrong thing, or just of the unknown. However, I can also see how it was figuratively the fear of human contact (of being known deeply). The very beginning of the contact is the focal point for this wider fear of meeting and being in relationship with strangers who often have a different skin color and (more than likely) cultural background. It makes me personally wonder if this struggle with introductions comes from a fear of "catching something" (i.e., change in culture/understanding/idealistic vision), or if it is more self-preservation in the form of spreading some "disease" (i.e., saying the wrong thing) that the person reacts viscerally to. I should say that this fear/struggle is mine too.

Apparently, the perceived threat rattles not only the community's sense of security and affinity for self-sameness. It is a threat that cuts to the core of their sense of identity and worth. Enduring contact with an "other" eventually requires a re-definition of who we are (identity), what we live by (values), and what we live for (vocation).

---

bringing the world toward the gospel. Mission is typically understood to be an expression of gospel-driven Christian service to the world. Recent literature on evangelism has encouraged churches to understand their "missional" work as evangelistic—it is witness through deed. Still others encourage the church to consider the ways in which the world is giving witness to God's saving work, which in turn might "convert" the church to its true calling. For this outside-in perspective on evangelism, see Cheri DiNovo, *Qu(E)Erying Evangelism: Growing a Community from the Outside In,* Center for Lesbian and Gay Studies in Religion and Ministry (Cleveland: Pilgrim Press, 2005).

Another pastor, Brody A., writes of this perceived threat to the fragility of small-town American identity:

> The church in which I serve is on the precipice of significant change. Having taken pride in its identity as a small, quaint, and rural farming community, [this congregation] is changing . . . and with that change, we find ourselves in the midst of an identity crisis. Housing developments have begun popping up all over the city. People from surrounding townships are moving to the area (especially younger families). Roads and infrastructure are being completely renovated as we prepare for a growth spike in the coming years. And caught in the midst of this change, I have witnessed local faith communities (including my own) struggling with what it means to be changed by the presence of "outsiders" who are now becoming part of the community. It is far too easy for people to "welcome" people into the area, but to keep them at arm's length. Risking human contact (friendships, relationships, and neighborliness mostly) means not only risking being changed by them, but risking the change in their very identity. For those who have always identified themselves as "small town folk," contact with these new members of the community threatens to shatter that identity they have cherished their whole lives.

In her response, United Methodist pastor Helen C. foregrounds the dimension of *race* for the collective White identity crisis:

> I've been thinking a lot about boundaries and identity lately. If we do not have a deep sense of our identity, it's difficult to understand our boundaries and limits. In terms of whiteness, I've found that white folk do not have a strong sense of identity beyond what is culturally prescribed. We talk about the invisibility of privilege, but I also think that for white folk (especially those who have adhered strongly to the societal scripts), their cultural identity is also cloaked in the process. For this reason, it is confusing and disorienting when they encounter the boundaries of groups with a strong identity [So they counter]: "We should all be able to get along!" "We accept everyone!" "All lives matter!"

Referring to the identity claims strategically deployed against counter-narratives that challenge dominant norms—for example, the rallying cry of "All Lives Matter" aimed at drowning out the justice-seeking demands of "Black Lives Matter"—Helen C. is detecting in her faith community the same tones of nostalgic anxiety heard in public discourse about the passing of "White Christian America."[40] These notes align with the reactionary patterns reportedly found in White Christian evangelicals and liberals. When confronted with statistical prophesies of their impending demise, a segment of White conserving evangelicals stokes "apocalyptic anger" with a staple of backward time-travel words—"reclaim," "restore," "renew," "repent," "revive."[41] Flaming nostalgic conflation of old-time religion with the "good old days," this fundamentalistic fervor for spiritual revival and repentance parallels an insistence upon so-called restoration (or maintenance) of the dominant status quo. Within this apocalyptic worldview, a nation is spiritually, socially, and politically "promiscuous" when its borders are porous to communicability with so-called aliens and strangers.

Good Christian liberals, on the other hand, display the tendency to retreat with guilt and shame, many wishing away their burden of White privilege and hoping that some form of cultural-ethnic reclamation (e.g., I am of Irish ancestry) might offer an alternative identity marker and heritage to replace the dreadful invisible power of whiteness.[42] For Shannon Sullivan, a scholar who has written extensively on the social construction of Whiteness, reactions of White shame, guilt, and fear revolve around variations of the ethic of love. On one hand, patterns of racial identity entrenchment (e.g., White supremacy) fuels a form of "oppositional love," and love of self that requires negation of the other. On the other hand, the strategies of racial identity denial (e.g., White guilt) easily lead to idealistic, unrealistic, and possibly repressive "multicultural love."[43] It is an eagerness to celebrate diversity and integrity, with the naïve assumption that the mixing of differences will naturally dissolve fears, increase empathy, and correct structural power imbalances. In effect, it does away with the necessity of risky contact.

---

40. Robert P. Jones, *The End of White Christian America* (New York: Simon & Schuster, 2016).

41. Ibid., 203.

42. Shannon Sullivan, *Good White People: The Problem with Middle-Class White Anti-Racism*, Suny Series, Philosophy and Race (Albany: SUNY Press, 2014), 117–18.

43. Ibid., 152–55.

When under threat of "catching something" new to its existing system, instead of casting it as foreign and alien, a community of faith might lean into a love different from the above forms, a kind of incarnational love that Sullivan tentatively calls "spiritually healthy self-love." Quite contrary to the notion of self-absorbing egocentrism, this is an outward-focused "transactional spiral,"[44] a reciprocal relationship, that allows a community to realize that contact with the other is vital to its very well-being. In terms of racial justice struggle, it means that White Christian communities garner the courage to transgress racial barriers because they recognize that such work saves not the lives of people of color, but rather their very own *White* lives.[45] Good liberal Christians would have to examine critically what it means to be entangled in the lives of those whom they consider to be the alien "other." On this point, Pastor Bruce J. is critically self-reflective: for him, the "other" might be an open-carry gun rights advocate, a non-religious person, a person of color, someone who is "not particularly well read on some sort of scholarship of the day even if they don't have a degree," a non-Christian. . . . For Pastor Brody A., a break-in of his church led this community of faith through a journey of experiencing shock and anger for having been violated, to acknowledging with pain the forces of poverty and violence that converge within this entanglement between them and the perpetrators (read their story below). Recalling the words of Dr. Martin Luther King Jr. on the interconnectedness of our collective fate as a human society, Pastor Conner D., planter of a predominantly African American, nondenominational congregation, offers these words:

> If we simply look at the iconic images of conflicts captured in Ferguson, Baton Rouge, and so forth, we see too often the full force of militarized policing brought to bear upon unarmed citizens. Armored personnel have virtually every inch of human flesh covered . . . a clear signal that human-to-human contact will not happen in this context. There is no wrestling because the clear signal has been sent . . . there will be no (fruitful) relationship. I cannot help but feel that militarized policing is emblematic of the struggles for fruitful community we face. Hearts and minds are covered in

44. Ibid., 159.

45. Ibid., 158–59.

the armaments of fear, hatred, and ignorance of the "other." There are too many clear signals that fruitful relationship is unwanted. And yet, as MLK told us, we have no choice in relationship . . . *either we live together as family or we perish together as fools.*[46]

Reflection question: How or where have you witnessed practices of LOVE ("[in]decent contact") that transformed contagious violence?[47]

Brody A.

A few months back, our church was hit with a series of break-ins. First it was the theft of our tool shed, where our lawn mower, weed-eater, and snowblower were taken. That alone shook up the congregation. Then, a few weeks later, we had a break-in of our actual building. Windows were smashed, doors were kicked down . . . I even had a fire extinguisher thrown through my office window. And what I noticed, despite the fact that this was not physical violence inflicted upon an individual, was that the church had experienced a violence of space. The congregation, who had for so long lived with this small-town mentality, could not come to grips with the idea that anyone would break into a church. It wasn't just hard to believe, but rather it was an impossibility that they simply could not comprehend. A lot of anger emerged from this series of events, and the contagious nature of violence rippled throughout the congregation. Many people wanted to react in the midst of their anger, wishing that "justice" would be served. What was once a "safe space" was now violated, and it would never be the same. However, together we processed our anger and our bitterness, and attempted to move forward with compassion and love. We offered prayers for

46. See Martin Luther King Jr., "Remaining Awake Through a Great Revolution" (commencement address, Oberlin College, June 1965), http://www.oberlin.edu/external/EOG/BlackHistoryMonth/MLK/CommAddress.html.

47. Reflection questions found in this and the subsequent two chapters were posed to my group of fourteen theological reflectors. Their responses are offered here as raw material—primary theologies—for readers' reflection. Consider using the questions from these chapters and the ministerial vignettes as material for group study.

the one who broke into our church, hoping that they were able to get what they needed, whatever that might have been. Instead of praying for justice, the attitude shifted, and we were praying for the ways in which systemic violence and poverty have pushed people to do such things, feeling like they have no other options left to them. Eventually donations and support came in from the outside community, as lawn mowers, snowblowers, and finances were donated to our church to help with the repairs. As our approach shifted from justice to compassion, it mirrored the way in which the surrounding community (outside of the church, no less) came together to help us in our time of need. It was beautiful to see the regenerative power of love firsthand.

Carnal Worship

The liturgical event narrated in chapter 1—the public liturgy of remembrance and repentance, organized by a group of multifaith leaders as Ferguson's Moral Monday in October 2014—revealed the power of human bodies to enact *carnal worship*. It is raw, earthy and earthly, fleshly embodied *leitourgia*, which, in breaking open the "thin spaces" between human and divine, between profane and sacred, draws the impossible closer to our reach. It is liturgy that performs the realm of God making it present right here on this fragile earth.

In the Christian lexicon, worship is liturgy—*leitourgia*, meaning "work of the people."[48] In the Hellenistic Mediterranean second-century BCE cultural context from whence the term came, *leitourgia* referred to the public work of civil leadership and service, which included a variety of civic and religious activities. Imported for Judeo-Christian usage, *leitourgia* came to signify within the eventual historical development of Christian worship the repertoire of religious ritualistic activities reserved for trained experts, and performed in religiously established settings.[49]

48. Maria Harris, *Fashion Me a People: Curriculum in the Church* (Louisville, KY: Westminster/John Knox Press, 1989), 95.

49. Mary Collins, "Principles of Feminist Liturgy," in *Women at Worship: Interpretations of North American Diversity,* ed. Marjorie Procter-Smith and Janet Roland Walton (Louisville, KY: Westminster John Knox Press, 1993), 18.

Essentially, good *leitourgia* came to be understood as patterns of order and meaning prescribed and enacted by those in religious authority.

Fortunately, several reformations or liturgical turns[50] occurred thanks to the risky innovations of contemporary feminist, womanist, and postcolonial theologians, who challenged the patriarchal, Eurocentric, and imperial logics that dictate the normative order and meaning for Christian liturgy. This work reminds us, first, that liturgy is fundamentally about human rituals that help give meaning to human relationship with one another and with the world. They "not only organize the religious life within sacred spaces or sanctuaries, but also interpret the life of the individual and the group in the world and consequently interpret the world itself. . . . Liturgical religious movements shape bodies, minds, spirits, politics, economies, and nation-states."[51]

Liturgy is about the ritualistic symbols and acts that help us to enact stories that confer transcendent meaning to life moments. And since human beings are ritualistic creatures, we constantly create rituals to socialize one another through various transitions of life:[52] birth, death, commitments, successes, failures, journeys, recollections, celebrations, grief, and so forth. As religious ritual, liturgy is where "the divine-human relationship is rehearsed and realized";[53] it is when a "human moment" is lifted up as paradigmatic, serving as the focal point upon which we can cast our "fears and hopes,"[54] and we remember that the divine is in covenant with us. Therein lies the power of a liturgical act as religious ritual: it allows us to perform our fears and hopes, and breaks open the possibility that the here-and-now can be transformed in a near future. In religious

50. Claudio Carvalhaes, ed. *Liturgy in Postcolonial Perspectives: Only One Is Holy* (New York: Palgrave Macmillan, 2015).

51. Ibid., 3.

52. Catherine M. Bell, *Ritual: Perspectives and Dimensions* (New York: Oxford University Press, 1997); cited in Collins, in *Women at Worship: Interpretations of North American Diversity.*

53. Herbert Anderson and Edward Foley, *Mighty Stories, Dangerous Rituals: Weaving Together the Human and the Divine* (San Francisco: Jossey-Bass, 1998).

54. Rosemary Radford Ruether, *Women-Church: Theology and Practice of Feminist Liturgical Communities* (San Francisco: Harper & Row, 1985), 107; cited in Charlotte Caron, *To Make and Make Again: Feminist Ritual Thealogy* [*sic*] (New York: Crossroad, 1993), 48–49.

educational terms, liturgy is an embodied curriculum that teaches us how to make sense of the world and how to act in it.

Given the profound meaning-making function of liturgy as religious ritual, many feminist, womanist, and postcolonial scholars have fought to reclaim the subversive, counter-hegemonic nature of Christian liturgy. This is the second insight to underscore. Liturgy is "communal ritualizing," and as such, it is "an active negotiation, construction, and production of relationships that both empower and set limits."[55] Consider the usual deliberations over familiar liturgies for worship and the two Protestant sacraments of baptism and Holy Communion: Who gets to preside? Who gets to participate? Who gets to write and say what words? From whence must our liturgical texts be retrieved? What are the proper orders of service? What are acceptable ritualistic symbols and gestures? What are the rules for determining orthopraxy—correct practice? Feminist/womanist and postcolonial liturgical theologians ardently resist orthodoxies that privilege oppressive norms that bar certain bodies from leadership and participation, norms that inscribe particular configurations of exclusive divine-human relationships (e.g., only men, only straight people, only Christians, only those without "sin" have access to God). Moreover, such theologians insist that subversive liturgy must be *insurrectional* and *resurrectional.* That is, it must bring back to life the stories, experiences, and expressions that have been subjugated[56] by dominant norms, and must participate in making sacred those lives rendered "unholy" by society. In doing so, liturgy offers healing, defined by Mary Farrell Bednarowski as the offering of hope: "individually and communally, to be healed is to have hope. To offer healing is to offer hope. And hope is that state wherein we know that some kind of response or change or reconciliation or transformation is possible."[57]

55. Collins, "Principles of Feminist Liturgy," 22.

56. Carvalhaes, *Liturgy in Postcolonial Perspectives*, 5. See also Michel Foucault, "Two Lectures," in *Power/Knowledge: Selected Interviews and Other Writings, 1972–1977*, ed. Colin Gordon (Brighton: Harvester, 1980).

57. Mary Farrell Bednarowski, "Our Work Is Change for the Sake of Justice: Hope Community, Minneapolis, Minnesota," in *Religion and Healing in America*, ed. Linda L. Barnes and Susan Starr Sered (Oxford: Oxford University Press, 2005), 195.

The liturgy enacted on that Moral Monday in October 2014 in Ferguson, Missouri, did just that.

> We are here to claim this public space as sacred space.
> we are here to declare sacred the actions already taken in Michael Brown's name
> we are here to consecrate the words already declared for Michael Brown, whose blood is still crying out in the streets
> . . .
> Today, our actions proclaim that our lives are sacred, our resistance is holy, and in the name of Michael Brown, Kajieme Powell, VonDerrit Myers, and all lives cut short by police brutality, this street is our sacred, holy space.
> We are challenged by the protesters who have courageously faced police every night, claiming this space by daring to imagine a world where blackness is not a weapon or a crime.
> . . .
> Because of this, we say: Whose street?
> Our street!
> Whose street?
> Our street![58]

It was a ritual that lifted up a human moment in which collective fears and hopes became entwined through word and act. It was a reclamation of the sacred worth and dignity of a life slain by systems of injustice, and a repossession of communal space defiled by insidious violence. It was a carnal expression of anguish in the language of the people, an act of fleshly defiance against organized forgetting (mentacide), and an earnest plea for recalibrated human relationships such that shields and weapons no longer demarcate the strictures of human contact. And with the foolishness of faith (1 Cor 1:18), it was an attempt to re-emplot a future in which the people's streets are no longer a death world, but rather a sacred, holy space. In all, it was also *leitourgia* in the original sense, as religious folk recog-

58. Liturgy written by students of Eden Theological Seminary. Used by permission.

nized that their liturgy did not end when their prayers were done. In fact, the "public work of the people" had just begun.

Not all efforts to ritualize the poignancy of human moments need be solemn. The combination of humor, aesthetics, and activism can be equally potent, as illustrated by "resistance rituals"[59] of the Women's Alliance for Theology, Ethics, and Ritual (WATER) during Holy Week of 1989.[60] Against the declaration of Washington, DC-area Catholic bishops that only men's feet would be washed on Maundy Thursday (because Jesus only washed the feet of male disciples!), the women staged stations of foot-washing outside the diocesan office and washed any and all feet with "bubble bath" and "plushy pink towels." On Good Friday morning, they participated with the Co-Madres march to protest US intervention in El Salvador; in the evening, they celebrated the stations of the cross by going to various embassies in the area to denounce violent actions perpetrated by different countries. On Holy Saturday they held silent fasting and lit the paschal fire. On Easter Sunday, they attended an art exhibit featuring Black women's photography and a performance of the Dance Theater of Harlem. On Monday, they went back to intervene in solidarity with the Co-Madres, because one of the women participating in the march had been deported.[61]

Christian religious ritual need not require fanciful expression. As illustrated by the stories shared by local clergy leaders, ritual can be moments in which expressions of communal grief allow a faith community to experience a touch of transcendence,[62] or it can be a series of intentional commitments repeated over time to expand (and even subvert) the repertoires of our liturgical traditions. In creative forms, carnal and incarnational worship beyond established settings and orders enhance our capacity for courageous communicability. Such *leitourgia* are dramaturgical lessons: they help communities

59. Dolores S. Williams, "Rituals of Resistance in Womanist Worship," in *Women at Worship: Interpretations of North American Diversity*, ed. Marjorie Procter-Smith and Janet Roland Walton (Louisville, KY: Westminster John Knox Press, 1993), 221.

60. Women's Alliance for Theology, Ethics, and Ritual, accessed February 1, 2017, www.waterwomensalliance.org/.

61. Caron, *To Make and Make Again*, 103–4.

62. See Mayra Rivera, *The Touch of Transcendence: A Postcolonial Theology of God* (Louisville, KY: Westminster John Knox Press, 2007).

of faith to enact a resurrectional, insurrectional reality, to stretch their capacity to see God's kin(g)dom being realized in their midst. Carnal worship teaches people of faith how to draw the impossible closer within reach.

Reflection question: How or where have you witnessed practices of "carnal worship," which enacts the realm of God as though it were right here on this fragile earth?

Matt B.

Many UU churches in the USA underwent widespread theological change after the merger of the Unitarian and the Universalist denominations, in 1961. For some (if not many) UU leaders, the theological liberalization of the traditions (and the new UUA as a whole) caused considerable controversy and contempt. Nevertheless, a fascinating feature of the liberalization has been the rapid influx of Pagan practitioners in many UU churches throughout the USA and Canada (Western/Eastern European and Indian practitioners tend to be more traditional, i.e., conservative in their theological orientation). The inclusion of Pagans in UU churches has, among many other things, generated dynamic and "fleshy" worship services that celebrate earth, seasonal harvests, spirit realms, and an overarching emphasis on the holiness of the body itself. Specific worship practices may include community harvesting/gardening, thanking/honoring one's body, and celebrating femininity as divine. These practices, on the whole, encourage participants to be thankful for the fragility of life itself, and the interdependent web of human existence; as the UUA continues to evolve, Pagans in our houses of worship serve as a powerful voice from the theological margins, demanding that our collective attentions never stray too far from the divine goddess and goddesses of everyday life.

Boundless Table

Regardless of form, at the heart of carnal Christian *leitourgia* is an invitation to a table, or more specifically, a meal. Liturgically, Christians recognize this ritual as Holy Communion, the Lord's Supper, or the Eucharist.[63] Theologically, many understand the Eucharist to be a meal of insurrection and resurrection. Developed over time, the Eucharist was derived from early Christian meal practices that were themselves an expression of "countersociety"—an enactment of a "meal world" that countered the social order inscribed by Hellenistic class-stratified associations and monitored by Roman imperial rule.[64] As Hal Taussig argues in his path-paving book *In the Beginning Was the Meal,* eating practices referenced throughout the New Testament attest to "a continuum [of] self-conscious social experimentation around issues of economic marginality, gender, and ethnic mix."[65] The Eucharistic meal takes on added layers of meaning, when counter-social and counter-economic meal practices, guided by the liturgy of Jewish prayers (for Passover or common meals), are combined with explicit remembrance of a crucifixion, an active remembering of "imperial punishment of insurrection."[66] A theological paradigm of counter-society for Christians today, the Eucharist as a Holy Meal scripts an "economy of grace [that] breaks through and transforms economic circumstances based on unjust distribution of food in a money-driven market economy."[67] Participation in this meal world becomes an act of communicable solidarity. In the blessing of the bread, we are "consecrating private property,"[68] acknowledging that what is considered ours really belongs to God. We remind one another that in God's abundance, there is enough for everyone, though not for accumulative storage (the story

63. Andrea Bieler and Luise Schottroff, *The Eucharist: Bodies, Bread, & Resurrection* (Minneapolis: Fortress Press, 2007), 103. *Eucharist* comes from the Greek verb *eucharistein,* "to give thanks."

64. Hal Taussig, *In the Beginning Was the Meal: Social Experimentation and Early Christian Identity* (Minneapolis: Fortress Press, 2009), 125–30.

65. Ibid., 170. Examples include the meal at which a woman anoints Jesus (Mark 14:3-9); the meal at the home of Martha and Mary (Luke 10:38-42); debates about the role of women at meal gatherings, which served as context for Paul's instructions about the Lord's Supper (1 Cor 11); controversies around Jews and Gentiles eating together (Gal 2:11-14); adjudications over divisive eating practices (Rom 14–15).

66. Taussig, *In the Beginning Was the Meal,* 130.

67. Bieler and Schottroff, *The Eucharist,* 84.

68. Ibid., 118.

of manna reminds us that). In remembering a crucified body as resurrected, we bear defiant witness to God's ultimate power over the violence of human tyranny.[69] In this alternative political economy—God's political economy—"sharing in the meal [means] sharing in justice, holiness, and communion."[70]

Yvonne K., minister of a multistaff, multiracial, LGBTQ-affirming congregation in St. Louis, witnessed a group of people—both churched and nonchurched volunteers—living out the paradigm of this "salvation economy." She also saw aggressive attempts at its obstruction.

> St. Louis Homeless Outreach is a group of concerned citizens who seek to meet the needs of those who are unhoused when winter and summer temperatures become life-threatening. In [the] summer of 2016, having heard multiple requests for food, outreachers began to distribute sandwiches and snacks along with ice water and Gatorade. Swiftly, police surveilling those who are unhoused approached outreachers with tickets, threatening arrest for those who dared to continue feeding their hungry kin. Feeding those who are unhoused resists the best efforts of developers, law enforcement, and policy-makers to complete colonization: displacing African American residents and businesses from Mill Creek Valley in the 1950s to create a new downtown that is for monied tourists, affluent loft-dwellers, and wealthy entrepreneurs. As Jesus did, outreachers feed masses of people in public for free, disrupting the capitalist economy that says only those with money deserve to live and occupy space. To the powerful, a salvation economy is a dangerous, infectious proposition. To block the infection, they have proposed Board Bill 66, the "Anti-Good Samaritan Bill" that criminalizes help to those who are unhoused and hungry. Jesus would surely have been threatened with arrest, too.[71]

In this instance, sharing sandwiches and Gatorade with unhoused sojourners becomes more than an act of patronizing charity for outreachers.

---

69. Ibid., 149.

70. Ibid., 120.

71. Facebook share, June 15, 2016, www.facebook.com/mo.costello.1/posts/10154197111139259; St. Louis Homeless Winter Outreach Facebook page, July 5, 2016, facebook.com/photo.php?fbid=10201733598138047&set=gm.10154325147684581&type=3&theater; Mill Creek Valley, accessed February 1, 2017, www.umsl.edu/virtualstl/phase2/1950/mapandguide/millcreeknode.html.

It is participating in communion with "hungry kin," an instantiation of risky communicability that defies barriers of state-sanctioned surveillance and quarantine.[72] It is not unlike the communion experienced when a historic suburban African American congregation pastored by Rev. Michael A. decided to open its doors and share a meal with protesters after the non-indictment of the White officer who fatally shot Michael Brown in Ferguson. Unsurprisingly, it was church folks who were "converted" by the holiness of new friendships forged in unlikely circumstances.

> My home church in a suburb of St. Louis opened its doors on Thanksgiving Day 2014 so that the protesters could have a meal and a safe place. The basement of the church started to become overcrowded and the worry of running out of food started to appear on the faces of the kitchen staff. More people continued to pour into the basement, but so did more food. The room was filled with diverse people both young and old, those born and raised in St. Louis as well as those far from home; those who were raised in the church as well as those who could be considered "unchurched." Some people sat at tables, others sat on the floor, and there were many standing against the wall, but everyone seemed to be deeply involved in the conversation with their neighbor and making room for others to join in. In the midst of multiple conversations taking place, one theme kept popping up: the love for one another. Many of the people gathered together probably would not have fellowshipped together under "normal" circumstances, but on that evening they put aside all the attention to their differences and focused on loving one another. But what stands out the most to me is that the people of the church seemed to have been more impacted by this coming together. Many of them did not understand why the protesters would come from [all] over the country, leaving the comforts of their homes. But through conversation and fellowship, they started to understand and appreciate those who were committed to the cause. Many friendships have been formed as a result of this shared meal.

The curriculum of eating—made paradigmatic in the Eucharist—teaches a community of faith two lessons, according to New Testament

72. To date, there is active organizing toward legal action should the measure passes by the vote of the city's board of aldermen; Camille Phillips, "Proposed St. Louis bill Would Require a License to Give to the Homeless," July 6, 2016, http://news.stlpublicradio.org/post/proposed-st-louis-bill-would-require-license-give-homeless#stream/0.

scholar Luise Schottroff and practical theologian Andrea Bieler: "sacramental permeability" and "eschatological imagination."[73] In religious educational language, these are lessons of yet another embodied curriculum, which, with the curricula of loving and praying, reinforce "that physical matters and actions such as eating and drinking can become vehicles that make transparent the Holy One who gives birth to the Eucharistic life." Indeed, the physical matters that symbolize our social and economic capital—our Communion tables, our dinner tables, the altars and spaces that we demarcate as safe and sacred for our communal practices—are a measure of either the boundlessness or the finitude of our capacity to live into God's economy of grace. They are a measure of our willingness to reorganize our way of life such that even ordinary, daily habits would contribute to the sustainable vitality for all. As additional stories from the local clergy below can attest, it takes but small acts to realize insurrectional, resurrectional hope, for each ordinary act is a *leitourgia* of everyday life, each echoing the words that invite Christians to the Eucharistic table: "come and let us weep together over the death and disasters of the world and the exclusion, pain, and hardships of our poor people; come and feast together on this table of promises, alterities, wisdom, and possibilities for a new world order."[74]

Reflection question: How or where have you witnessed table practices that dismantle the barriers of surveillance and quarantine, such that what and how we eat become the "contagion" that heals?

Brody A.

When I was called to be the pastor of this congregation, one of the responsibilities in my contract was to serve on the board of directors of a local nonprofit called Community Care (http://nrcommcare.org/). . . . Community Care is an organization that started off in the basement of two local churches . . . and has grown exponentially to serve the entire city of North Ridgeville and the

73. Bieler and Schottroff, *The Eucharist*, 5.

74. Carvalhaes, *Liturgy in Postcolonial Perspectives*, 17.

> surrounding communities. Its main purpose is to provide food assistance to those who are lacking the resources they need to feed their families, but it also helps with clothing, utility assistance, and essential items (such as toothpaste, deodorant, soap, etc.). Recently Community Care has shifted their focus with their food assistance program, focusing on healthier options that many of our clients are not able to receive [normally]. Starting a "summer salad program," we invited not just those in need of food assistance but the seniors of the community as well to come receive free salad mix and ingredients every week during the summer. We recognized that both the senior citizens of the community and those who need food assistance are less likely to receive healthy food options, as processed food and unhealthy food is far cheaper and more accessible. Focusing on healing their bodies with nourishing food, we believe that we can make an impact that spreads beyond the tables in their homes. Additionally, having both the senior citizens and those who are in need of assistance come to the center to get their salad every week puts them in physical proximity with one another. Over time they have developed friendships with one another, as the senior citizens are becoming more and more open and friendly with people they would have looked down upon at the beginning of the year.

The vignettes shared in this chapter offer testimonies of practices of (in)decent contact, carnal liturgical innovation, and boundless table. They are exemplars of what it means to imagine ministerial praxis in the light of Jesus's very public curricula of eating, praying, and loving. A community configured by such communicability is one that moves closer to *redeemability*—a capacity to recognize the promises of gospel and to participate in making good on those promises. For this exploration, we turn to chapter 5.

Chapter 5

Practicing Redeemability

"[Two] years later, Ferguson protests have produced some change," wrote Stephen Deere of the *St. Louis Post-Dispatch* on August 7, 2016, two days before the two-year anniversary of the shooting death of Michael Brown.[1] A retrospective in conjunction with other commemorative events organized throughout St. Louis on the occasion of the anniversary, the article delineated how the actions of "a new generation of demonstrators" two years ago have affected the beginning of positive change for this small St. Louis County suburb and its disenfranchised citizenry. Among the results: a Department of Justice investigation of the Ferguson Police Department and Municipal Court, which yielded a report containing excoriating details of a system of racial-profiling, race-targeting, revenue-generating policing; the departure of more than twenty police officers, and the selection of a new police chief, a new city manager, and four new city council members; the appointment by Missouri governor Jay Nixon of a sixteen-member Ferguson Commission,[2] which held a painstaking, participatory self-study of the St. Louis region and produced a "198-page report with

1. Stephen Deere, "2 Years Later, Ferguson Protests Have Produced Some Change," *St. Louis Post-Dispatch*, August 7, 2016, www.stltoday.com/news/local/crime-and-courts/years-later-ferguson-protests-have-produced-some-change/article_7cd4d141-e912-5893-83d8fecee2d6922d.html. Memorial vigils and protests took place throughout the weekend, leading up to August 9, 2016; Steve Giegerich, Kristen Taketa, and Nancy Cambria, "Gunfire Mars Solemn Day of Second Anniversary of Michael Brown's Death," *St. Louis Post-Dispatch*, August 10, 2016, www.stltoday.com/news/local/metro/vigil-and-silence-mark-the-second-anniversary-of-michael-brown/article_9128e099-92c8-506c-a2e9-f52b7ada1b35.html.

2. STL Positive Change, accessed February 1, 2017, https://stlpositivechange.org/.

189 'calls to action,'" including recommendations such as "ending predatory lending and poverty, improving training for officers, consolidating police departments and municipal courts, and providing equitable access to rigorous courses in high school."[3] The work recommended by the Ferguson Commission will be monitored by a nonprofit board called Forward through Ferguson.[4]

"It's going to take individuals, and communities, and systems working together collectively to do this. And that's a paradigm shift."[5] The words of Bethany Johnson-Javois, managing director of the Ferguson Commission, echo the wisdom known too well by those committed to working toward enduring social change. Whatever results have been seen thus far are but the beginning of a long haul, and they would simply be cosmetic or Band-Aid solutions to systemic problems unless there is a paradigm shift. Johnson-Javois's words reflect an "educated hope,"[6] an ethical imagination that sees the long arc of struggle to re-organize collective values, commitments, and resources toward the realization of a more just community. They also reflect the fundamental human conviction that the broken world in which we live is *redeemable.* It *must* and *does* get better,[7] it can be reconfigured, we tell one another, and by such galvanizing words we gain courage to live in a "not-yet" reality as though a better future has already arrived.

---

3. Deere, "2 Years Later," www.stltoday.com/news/local/crime-and-courts/years-later-ferguson-protests-have-produced-some-change/article_7cd4d141-e912-5893-83d8-fecee2d6922d.html.

4. Forward through Ferguson, accessed February 1, 2017, http://forwardthroughferguson.org/; See also Jim Wallis, *America's Original Sin: Racism, White Privilege, and the Bridge to a New America* (Grand Rapids: Brazos Press, 2016), 15–24.

5. "What Comes Next," STL Positive Change, accessed February 1, 2017, https://stlpositivechange.org/commission-work/whats-next.

6. Henry A. Giroux, *The Violence of Organized Forgetting: Thinking beyond America's Disimagination Machine,* City Lights Open Media (San Francisco: City Lights Books, 2014), 83–84.

7. The It Gets Better Project is a now a worldwide movement that was started in 2010 by an inspirational message created by columnist Dan Savage with his partner Terry Miller, in response to the surge of anti-gay bullying and its devastating effect on lesbian, gay, bisexual, and transgender youth; see It Gets Better, accessed August 9, 2016, www.itgetsbetter.org/pages/about-it-gets-better-project/.

Redemption is not simply a Christian theological imperative. Even more fundamentally, across cultures and time, "the Human Being is a repairing animal," writes philosopher Elizabeth V. Spelman in her book *Repair: The Impulse to Restore in a Fragile World*.[8] The repair work ranges from mechanical to medical, relational to social, psychological to environmental; and the brokenness, decay, or destruction that compel mending can be consequences of everyday wear and tear, or violent "deliberate destruction" that leaves "ruins."[9] Spelman calls to mind the wide range of repair words in the English vocabulary: "renewal, redemption, reconciliation, salvation, compensation, consolation, resilience, restoration, repair; to heal, mend, recover, rebuild, resolve, reconstruct."[10] Lodging repair "at the very heart of justice,"[11] Spelman discusses the range of restorative options with case studies of historic injuries—from the work of truth and reconciliation in South Africa, to exploration of reparations for slavery in the United States, internment of Japanese Americans, and the genocide of Native Americans and First Nations communities in the United States and Canada. "Repair is the creative destruction of brokenness"—it reveals the "mutability and impermanence" of our world.[12] At the same time, the *Homo reparans* knows that some forms of brokenness are beyond reparation, and some things are more beautiful when left unmended.[13]

The Christian faith community also understands repair to be at the heart of justice, and we have multiple traditions from which to draw our own rather eclectic lexicon of repair work. Most familiar are activities that framed the ministry of Jesus: bringing good news to the poor, releasing the captives, healing infirmities, letting the oppressed go free, proclaiming God's Jubilee.[14] Or, with brutal honesty: "digging up and pulling down,"

8. Elizabeth V. Spelman, *Repair: The Impulse to Restore in a Fragile World* (Boston: Beacon Press, 2002), 1.

9. Ibid., 103, 105.

10. Ibid., 121.

11. Ibid., 51.

12. Ibid., 8, 134.

13. Ibid., 132–33.

14. Luke 4:18-19.

"destroying and demolishing," "building and planting."[15] More poetically inspirational are calls to let justice roll down like waters, mend broken walls, restore livable streets. No matter the range of activity, our faith traditions insist that restorative work must mend individuals and communities and fuse the personal with the political. New Testament scholar Melanie Johnson-DeBaufre calls this a historical, literary, and theological trajectory of "utopian social dreaming," in which such ideals as the "kin(g)dom of God"—*basileia tou theou*—help to animate imagination for possible new worlds.[16] Not only that, the biblical utopian dream is often framed in earnest archeological and ecological terms, a reminder that the restoration of death worlds requires not only the infrastructures of justice but also an ecosystem that yields vitality to life, from generation to generation:

> You will be like a watered garden,
>   like a spring of water that won't run dry.
> They will rebuild ancient ruins on your account;
>   the foundations of generations past you will restore.
> You will be called Mender of Broken Walls,
>   Restorer of Livable Streets.[17]

Christian religious education, says practical theologian Mary C. Boys, is about facilitating processes through which people can "realize the world is in need of repair," "believe that something can be done to repair it," and "form a community of persons who sustain each other in the work of repairing."[18] In this vein, I suggest two dimensions of faithful repair work that conjoin the individual with the communal, the personal with the political, to imagine the potency of social dreaming for the sake of

---

15. Jeremiah 1:10.

16. Melanie Johnson-DeBaufre, Catherine Keller, and Elias Ortega-Aponte, eds., *Common Goods: Economy, Ecology, and Political Theology*, Transdisciplinary Theological Colloquia (New York: Fordham University Press, 2015), 103–23.

17. Isaiah 58:11-12.

18. Mary C. Boys, "The Tradition as Teacher: Repairing the World," *Religious Education* 85, no. 3 (1990): 346–55; see also Jack L. Seymour, "The Clue to Christian Religious Education: Uniting Theology and Education, 1950 to the Present," *Religious Education* 99, no. 3 (2004): 276.

twenty-first-century utopias. These two dimensions have to do with the kind of repair that Christians call redemption, or what theologian David Kelsey calls "making up" and "making good": first, we consider what it would take to realize that the world is in need of repair—what I call resurrectional consciousness; and, second, what it would take to express that something can and must be done about it—what I call insurrectional witness. A community conscientized to this work would come to understand its redeeming capacity—*redeemability*—and would be called to live fully into its redemptive capabilities.

Resurrectional Consciousness: Seeing Things as They Could/ Should Be

On December 17, 2010, twenty-six-year-old Tunisian fruit vendor Mohamed Bouazizi set himself on fire in alleged protest against a humiliating encounter with local law enforcement, and his death was quickly branded by media outlets as what triggered the revolutionary "Arab Spring."[19] Despite conflicting recollections of his encounter with police, and the usual muddied speculations about his motivation, Bouazizi's self-immolation became a haunting symbol of a people's pain and rage under global economic crisis.[20] The ensuing populist uprisings across North Africa and the Middle East—dubbed the Arab Spring—marked a resurgence of the masses against oppressive political and economic regimes. Once again, global superpowers were reminded that "the protester" will

---

19. Kareem Fahim, "Slap to a Man's Pride Set Off Tumult in Tunisia," *The New York Times*, January 21, 2011, www.nytimes.com/2011/01/22/world/africa/22sidi.html?_r=1&pagewanted=2&src=twrhp; Thessa Lageman, "Mohamed Bouazizi: Was the Arab Spring Worth Dying For?" *Aljazeera*, January 3, 2016, www.aljazeera.com/news/2015/12/mohamed-bouazizi-arab-spring-worth-dying-151228093743375.html; Joerg Rieger and Pui-lan Kwok, *Occupy Religion: Theology of the Multitude*, Religion in the Modern World (Lanham, MD: Rowman & Littlefield Publishers, 2012), 2.

20. Elizabeth Day, "The Slap That Sparked a Revolution," *The Guardian*, May 14, 2011, www.theguardian.com/world/2011/may/15/arab-spring-tunisia-the-slap.

not resign to a repressive state, but would demonstrate outrage by means outside of political processes that are denied to them.[21]

Insurgence against economic disparity in the United States found expression in the Occupy Wall Street movement, in which Zuccotti Park of New York City became a tent-city occupied by protesters who rallied for the interests of "the 99 percent."[22] Dismissed at first as a purpose-less and leader-less non-movement, the occupiers of Zuccotti Park and other tent-cities across the country argued for a new kind of efficacy in supposedly disorderly public actions of the people *en masse.* Theologians Joerg Rieger and Kwok Pui-lan see the Occupy and Arab Spring movements, along with the subsequent Black Lives Matter (BLM) movement sparked in 2012 by the killing of Trayvon Martin,[23] as instantiations of the power of "the multitude."[24] Like other movements of previous generations (e.g., Latin American liberation, feminist, Black Power, and the *minjung* struggle in South Korea), these recent movements signal for Rieger and Kwok the enduring power of the people to act collectively as an active "political subject"[25] animated by awakened political consciousness. For public intellectuals like Cornel West, the "democratic awakening and accountability" demonstrated by the Occupy protesters is a resurrection of the spirit of previous change-makers such as the Rev. Martin Luther King Jr., Dorothy Day, Dolores Huerta, and Cesar Chavez.[26]

This is the first powerful dimension of repair work: a capacity for *resurrectional consciousness.* Here, we don't focus on the people's actions yet; rather, we focus on the nature of their awakened consciousness—a state in which they are able to recognize and articulate that their world is in need

21. "The Protester" was chosen as *Time*'s "Person of the Year" in 2011, accessed August 9, 2016, http://content.time.com/time/person-of-the-year/2011/.

22. "2011: A Year in Revolt," *Occupy Wall Street,* January 3, 2012, http://occupywallst.org/article/2011-year-revolt/.

23. Black Lives Matter, accessed February 1, 2017, http://blacklivesmatter.com/.

24. Rieger and Kwok, *Occupy Religion,* 6.

25. Rieger and Kwok, citing the work of political theorists Michael Hardt and Antonio Negri. See *Empire* (Cambridge, MA: Harvard University Press, 2000).

26. Rieger and Kwok, *Occupy Religion,* 41.

of repair, an awareness facilitated by their coming together in critical mass, and an awareness that resurrects hope for social change.

First, social movements such as the Arab Spring, Occupy Wall Street, and Black Lives Matter illustrate the power of resurrectional consciousness. Through strategies unconventional and sometimes un-choreographed,[27] "the multitude" demonstrates a refusal to accept the "living death"[28] that unjust social systems perpetuate. It is an "emergent" consciousness, a kind of "expectancy," which the Brazilian educational philosopher Paulo Freire described as dispositions necessary for radical change.

In his revolutionary text *Pedagogy of the Oppressed*, Freire declares that "education is suffering from narration sickness."[29] Colonized by a "banking approach" (as discussed in chapter 2), public (and religious) education under repressive social policies has become a "lifeless and petrified" narration of the world, because the *word* that is being taught and the *world* that it signifies have been rendered "motionless, static, compartmentalized, and predictable."[30] Learners subjected to the banking approach are treated as mere "spectator" in the world, docile recipients of knowledge deposited into them from higher authorities, rather than as "re-creators" "*with* the world and with others."[31] The banking approach extinguishes learners' capacity to be subjects with historical agency; they are assumed to be bereft or are intentionally stripped of any notion that they could possibly intervene in larger social, cultural, political forces that would alter their reality for the better.[32]

27. It is important to note here that we must take care to avoid romanticizing "unconventional," as though it were inherently virtuous and revolutionary. Additionally, I do not consider acts of self-harm to have redemptive value. It is a form of violence that is the base of unhelpful and harmful logics underlying the religious categories of "sacrifice" and "redemptive violence."

28. Paulo Freire, *Pedagogy of the Oppressed*, trans. Myra Bergman Ramos, new rev. 20th-anniversary ed. (New York: Continuum, 1997), 113, 52.

29. Ibid., 52.

30. Ibid., 52.

31. Ibid., 56.

32. Ibid., 62.

The revolutionary alternative to "banking" is *conscientização*, conscientization, or consciousness-raising through "critical thinking and the quest for mutual humanization."[33] Conscientization equips learners with the capacity for problem-posing, to tune their attention to the situations and conditions that limit their freedom to participate in the world. Freire insists, "Whereas banking education anesthetizes and inhibits creative power, problem-posing education involves a constant unveiling of reality. The former attempts to maintain the *submersion* of consciousness; the latter strives for the *emergence* of consciousness and *critical intervention* in reality."[34]

Here, we reformulate Freire's notion of emergent critical consciousness as *resurrectional* because it marks a refusal to let death-dealing systems have the final word on the state of the world. When narration sickness produces false narratives—such as that the 99 percent are takers, the Arab world is devoid of democracy, Black lives don't matter—then resurrectional consciousness prompts vehement rejection of such lies. After all, the Christian faith is built upon such resurrectional imagination: the outright refusal to let death-dealing imperial power have the final say against hope. Christians proclaim, Jesus may have been executed by a colonial empire, and his death sanctioned by a corrupt religious system, but he lives, and his spirit is in the multitude. Such proclamation of resurrectional hope is born out of the ability to see reality not as it is, but as it could and should be.

Resurrectional hope is evident in the emergent consciousness of social uprisings, and this seems to be a case in which Christian faith communities are converted by that hope that is animating actions outside of church walls. Sometimes, faith communities lead the action toward social change; sometimes, faith communities practice active followership with baby steps, but those "little moves" and "small acts" are what it takes to overcome the drag of inertia.[35]

33. Ibid., 55–56.

34. Ibid., 62. Italics in original.

35. Peter Ochs, "Small Actions against Terror: Jewish Reflections on a Christian Witness," in *Surviving Terror: Hope and Justice in a World of Violence*, ed. Victoria Lee Erickson and Michelle Lim Jones (Grand Rapids: Brazos Press, 2002); Nancy E. Bedford, "Little Moves

When asked about evidence of resurrectional imagination within the local faith community, pastor Michael A. shares the story of his congregation's ginger steps toward awakened consciousness with another neighborhood congregation that is in many ways dissimilar to them. His historic African American congregation and another predominantly White suburban congregation had been existing in geographic proximity, yet they shared no joint experience or tradition, nor any pressing need to interact. Suddenly, jolted by the actions in the streets and in other faith communities surrounding them, they reached out to each other with curiosity. Michael A. writes,

> [We] are two different congregations in terms of faith tradition, historical experience, and demographic composition. Yet both churches desire to see improvements in their shared suburban community and therefore are developing a partnership.
>
> Methodist and Unitarian congregations do not normally worship together, [we] have had one joint worship service [over in their space] with [community leader] Bethany Johnson-Javois serving as the guest speaker. The worship service centered around the Ferguson Commission Report and passionate service. After the worship service, we broke out into several groups to discuss some of the recommendations in the report.
>
> A few months later on a Friday evening, the two churches came together again, over a spaghetti dinner with sub sandwiches that was held in the lower level of [my church]. Though the space quickly became cramped due to the large number of people in attendance, the two congregations were able to fellowship together. After the meal, attendees shared their sense of purpose or a fun fact about themselves. It has been interesting to witness a small, predominantly black Methodist congregation and a large, predominantly white Unitarian congregation seem eager to collaborate.
>
> Time will tell whether the practices of eating and praying together of these two congregations will lead them closer together toward the paradigm shift that community leader Bethany Johnson-Javois envisions. But their example, as well as the actions that multitudes have initiated across the country and the globe, give witness to the power of social dreaming, which makes repair work possible.

---

against Destructiveness: Theology and the Practice of Discernment," in *Practicing Theology: Beliefs and Practices in Christian Life*, ed. Miroslav Volf and Dorothy C. Bass (Grand Rapids: W. B. Eerdmans, 2002).

Stacey A.

The women I worked with who experienced physical and/or sexual violence are the very embodiment of a "not yet" reality; their full bodies are daily engaged in small acts of resilience and survival that create/build the muscle of a new life. Each day of agreeing to re-engage with the world, when they are still experiencing violence, is resurrectional. . . . Wald's work on contagions in the world and Spelman's on being "repairing animals" recalled for me an example of their shared work of repair. In group art therapy, one exercise asks the women to draw unhealthy then healthy boundaries. They imagine a cell in their body which had no boundaries from violence, and in the other image they are asked to imagine cells rebuilding healthy barriers and allowing in the nourishment of love, faith, friendship, and care. The conversations that follow after this exercise inevitably bring about not only testimony of what the body and mind can endure, but they empower one another with stories of how love and hope can bring equilibrium back (at a metaphorically cellular level).

Insurrectional Witness: Witnessing Truth to Power

The 2008 decision of The UMC to add "witness" to its liturgical profession of membership, alongside prayers, presence, gifts, and service, reflects the historic Christian understanding that the Christian faith community is one called to *marturia—to* "bear witness."[36] For contemporary ears, witness connotes robust missional and evangelistic activities. What often gets left out is the extent to which the faithful in earlier eras of Christian history had to bear witness, sometimes "even unto death."[37] Such witness is public and costly.

36. Thomas H. Groome, *Will There Be Faith? A New Vision for Educating and Growing Disciples* (New York: HarperOne, 2011), 165.

37. I also do not suggest that we attempt to make sense of the suffering and death of contemporary social victims in terms of martyrdom. If treated uncritically, such facile association runs the risk of valorizing suffering and reinforcing a harmful redemptive logic to violence.

Christian religious educational scholarship has also debated these two facets of witness by attending to the tensions of discipleship and citizenship. As sociologist John A. Coleman once put it, "The *church that educates for discipleship must also educate for citizenship.*"[38] These two interrelated tasks ensure that the work of faith formation always supposes a public faith—a faith characterized by publicly evident commitment to a principled way of life that is organized by one's "utopian social dreaming" for the realization of God's kin(g)dom on earth.[39] Such a principled public faith is costly, because it has to endure "*a taxing reality test,* an experiential proving ground for Christian claims for a this-worldly, liberative, regenerative potential in grace and redemption."[40] A public faith is one that dares to declare—even at cost to self—that societal brokenness is reparable. We hear this expressed through the axiom "speaking truth to power." Keeping with resurrectional consciousness, we might call this the capacity to incite, and even insurrect, witness-bearing against the powers that be, as modeled by the *marturia* of the protesting multitude.

Protest as Witness

Recent protest movements raise again the question of why or how protests are necessary and efficacious within a democratic society that supposedly provides multiple avenues for political participation. One definition of protest activity is as follows: it is "a mode of political action oriented toward objection to one or more policies or conditions, characterized by showmanship or display of an unconventional nature, and undertaken to obtain rewards from political or economic systems while working within the systems."[41] The term *reward* may trigger negative association with

38. John A. Coleman, "The Two Pedagogies: Discipleship and Citizenship," in *Education for Citizenship and Discipleship,* ed. Mary C. Boys (New York: Pilgrim Press, 1989), 57. Italics in original text.

39. Coleman described discipleship as a modeling of the Christian life on "the decisive dispositions of Jesus," the "crucial paradigmatic actions in Jesus' life," and "a utopian teaching related to the realm of God. . . ." Ibid., 45.

40. Ibid., 60.

41. Roberta Ann Johnson, "Mobilizing the Disabled," in *Waves of Protest: Social Movements since the Sixties,* ed. Jo Freeman and Victoria L. Johnson, People, Passions, and Power (Lanham, MD: Rowman & Littlefield Publishers, 1999), 32.

self-serving interests, when we could understand it more generically as intent on seeking reaction or return. Protests take on different forms, from individualistic to collective, from dissociative (isolating from the system) to oppositional confrontation. Protest actions like that of civil disobedience are "open and public defiance[s] of accepted law or norm[s], undertaken purposefully with the intent of altering state policy."[42]

Analyzing the characteristics of social movement organizations since the 1960s, Jo Freeman suggests that protest actions become a social movement when there exist the following elements: a "preexisting communications network" with people and resources to ensure endurance and continuity of activity; a flexibility to fold new issues into the existing umbrella network; "a series of crises that galvanize" people in the network into action; and "subsequent organizing effort to weld the spontaneous groups together into a movement."[43] From this framework and other studies, we extract the following features of protest movements:

1. they build upon the momentum and wisdom of preexisting networks;
2. they turn crises into opportunities for consciousness-raising;
3. they ignite collective empowerment for strategic use of confrontation;
4. they are open to multiple and interactive forms, expressions, and leadership.

First, protest movements mobilize and organize into preexisting networks of people and resources that provide the mechanisms for communicating desired messages. The efficacy lies in strategic collective action and deployment of collective resources. In short, no single protester is effective standing alone. Rosa Parks's act of civil disobedience on a bus in Montgomery in 1955 is often depicted simply as a brave act of a tired citizen, but that

42. David S. Meyer, *The Politics of Protest: Social Movements in America* (New York: Oxford University Press, 2007), 103.

43. Jo Freeman, "On the Origins of Social Movements," in Freeman and Johnson, *Waves of Protest,* 19–20.

singular act influenced a movement because Parks was connected to the well-established NAACP and the Highlander Folk School's leadership programs.[44]

Second, protest movements turn crises into events that precipitate consciousness-raising action. In her study of race riots, Ann Collins points out that all riots are traceable to some precipitating event(s)[45]—a shooting death of a Black youth in the case of Ferguson in 2014; or a gunfire between Whites, Blacks, and an unmarked police car that triggered the East St. Louis riot in 1917; or an act of self-immolation that catalyzed the rise of the Arab Spring.[46] When precipitating events "crystalize and focus discontent," people are incited to take up direct, concrete action.[47] But individual commitment is sustained only when there is strategic consciousness-raising about the issues that compel continuous action. Sometimes, minds are changed through action, and the work becomes more effective. In this sense, the painstaking work of the Ferguson Commission's public forms, and the numerous teach-ins, preach-ins, and eat-ins that have been organized by local activists and religious groups since 2014, make up this necessary matrix of community conscientization.

Third, protest movements make strategic use of confrontation. Public actions invite bodies to become both medium and message. Aside from the strategically choreographed standoffs between protesters and law enforcement, there are also clever uses of collective bodies in ways that electrify the sense of collective identity. The "people's mic" of the Occupy movement is one such example; instead of bullhorns, human voices amplified public messages.[48] Images of protesters with locked arms marching down

44. Meyer, *The Politics of Protest*, 176–77.

45. Ann V. Collins, *All Hell Broke Loose: American Race Riots from the Progressive Era through World War II*, Praeger Series on American Political Culture (Santa Barbara, CA: Praeger, 2012).

46. Elliott M. Rudwick, *Race Riot at East St. Louis: July 2, 1917* (Cleveland, OH: Meridian Books, 1966).

47. Freeman, "On the Origins of Social Movements," 21–22.

48. Carrie Kahn, "Battle Cry: Occupy's Messaging Tactics Catch On," December 6, 2011, www.npr.org/2011/12/06/142999617/battle-cry-occupys-messaging-tactics-catch-on.

main streets remain the enduring emblem of the multitude taking a stand for what they believe in.

Finally, protest movements take different forms and expressions—marches, vigils, sit-ins, die-ins, occupying tactics, and now in particular the widespread use of social media.[49] The use of social media since the Arab Spring has particularly reinforced the collapse of context and time for public action. Technology now allows the multitude to create their own new spaces, new usage of time, and new ways of mobilizing specialized and unspecialized resources.[50] Cell phone cameras have become powerful devices for a new wave of guerilla recording and dissemination of evidence of violent confrontations between citizens and law enforcement.

From the above general characteristics of protest movements, we draw analogies for the understanding of Christian *marturia*, public witness-bearing of faith.

First, public witness is collective. It is less about individual evangelists testifying to friends and co-workers the power of their faith in their everyday life, no matter how powerful that form of witness may be. Rather, here we are focusing on the witness of *ekklesia*—the church as "assembly," a term connoting political and religious characteristics within the context of Hellenistic Judaism.[51] Numerous theologians have proffered powerful constructs for our renewed understanding of church that defies repressive confines of space and time.[52] Here, we are reminded that the power of faith lies in the kinesthetic energy of the multitude.

49. For helpful critiques of the colonial connotation of the expression "occupy," see Rieger and Kwok, *Occupy Religion*, 45.

50. Freeman, "A Model for Analyzing the Strategic Options of Social Movement Organizations," in *Waves of Protest*, 223–27. The "pink hat" project that was part of the Women's March on January 21, 2017, gives evidence to the enduring creativity of protest movements. The creators of the project envisioned a sea of pink hats knitted and adorned by marchers, an assertion of the aesthetic and symbolic power of women in the fabric of society. See www.pussyhatproject.com/.

51. Rieger and Kwok, *Occupy Religion*, 112–13.

52. See the notion of "ecclesia-in-transit" in HyeRan Kim-Cragg and Mai-Anh Le Tran, "Turning to the Other: Interdenominational, Interethnic, Interreligious Activism and a New Ecclesia," in *Complex Identities in a Shifting World: Practical Theological Perspectives*, ed. Robert Mager, Pamela Couture, Pamela McCarroll, and Natalie Wigg-Stevenson (Zurich: Lit Verlag

Second, public witness is needed in times of crises, especially crises of meaning. When existing paradigms of reality prove inadequate to explain the disrepair of the world, a new word is needed to breathe life into dry bones (Ezek. 37:1-14). Crises are also opportunities for educative conscientization in the Freirean sense. The initiation into activism described by David Meyer is strikingly similar to how individuals might be initiated into public faith:

> Becoming an activist is rarely the result of a dramatic moment of conversion; rather, it is an ongoing process in which an individual comes to see himself or herself as a member of a larger group, one whose efforts might make a difference politically and give meaning to a life. Activists come from, and join into, strong social networks that organize much of what they do.[53]

Third, the Christian faith has deep roots in confrontation, specifically head-on confrontations with imperial and religious power. In their evocative book *The Last Week*, Marcus Borg and John Dominic Crossan challenge us to reimagine the "triumphal entry" of Jesus into Jerusalem as one of a peasant's counter-protest against the ominous imperial procession of Caesar.[54] Borg and Crossan depict the contrast: "Pilate's procession embodied the power, glory, and violence of the empire that ruled the world. Jesus's procession embodied an alternative vision, the kingdom of God"—an end of chariots, war horses, battle bows.[55] To understand faith as public marturia today is to understand the spirit of that first-century movement, in which a motley of ordinary people used their bodies for utopian social dreaming.

Finally, public witness today can take multiple creative forms and patterns, as was the way of Jesus and his peasant's revolt. We saw a great example of such creativity from the organizers and participants of the United Methodist Women's (UMW) National Seminar, held at the University

---

GmbH & Co. KG Wien, 2015). Rieger and Kwok point to the work of Letty Russell, Dietriech Bonhoeffer, Leonardo Boff, Brian McLaren.

53. Meyer, *The Politics of Protest*, 3.

54. Marcus J. Borg and John Dominic Crossan, *The Last Week: The Day-by-Day Account of Jesus's Final Week in Jerusalem* (San Francisco: HarperSanFrancisco, 2006), 2.

55. Ibid., 4.

of Illinois in Chicago on July 29–August 2, 2015, under the theme "Interrupting Indifference: Jesus, Justice and Joy." Their witness paralleled the aforementioned WATER collective's actions. Over the course of five days, about two hundred women participated in worship, workshops, site visits, and a town hall/rally event to gain deeper insight into four sets of social justice issues: "climate change, economic injustice, mass incarceration, and maternal and child health."[56] An impromptu gesture of solidary turned into an act of quiet protest when a small group of women decided to show up with makeshift signs at a hearing at Cook County Hospital (which serves lower-income communities of color) to oppose the closing of its neonatal unit. Their decision came about after having learned in a plenary about the effects of racism, sexism, and poverty on the health of racial/ethnic women and babies.[57] The action was improvisational and paled in comparison to other organized activities. However, it was an important direct and concrete action for this particular group, because they had been conscientized to the gravity of the issue; they had been inspired by the stories of activists young and old who testify to the power of collective action for structural change; and just days earlier they had playfully dramatized Jesus's peasant revolt by turning the biblical story of the triumphal entry into a protest march, while singing words to the tune "Enter into Jerusalem."

Marturia—witness-bearing—is insurrectional because of our insistence that the brokenness of creation is redeemable. I have insisted that it is public and collective; it is *leitourgia*—public ritual—as much as it is political confrontation. All that aside, I would like to leave room for arguments that a personal act can also be public, and part and parcel of collective action. The repertoire of Christian practices includes one activity that seems to blend *leitourgia* with *marturia*—and that is the activity of *prayer*.

What if we were to imagine prayer as protest?

---

56. Yvette Moore, "United Methodist Women Act for Justice at National Seminar," United Methodist Women, August 1, 2015, www.unitedmethodistwomen.org/news/nationalseminar2015wrap.

57. See the PBS documentary series *Unnatural Causes*, episode 2, "When the Bough Breaks," www.unnaturalcauses.org/episode_descriptions.php?page=2.

Prayer as Protest

According to Priscilla Wald, communicable diseases do not just reveal human fear and misgivings about contact. They also reveal some positive aspects of human community: that we are inextricably interdependent; we are resilient and resourceful in efforts toward healing; and we believe that "healing" is spiritual, even when we are dealing with biological diseases. This last point is fascinating: as Wald sees it, there is a mystifying "superstitious" dimension to human apprehensions about diseases—sometimes in defiance of clear science, often driven by ignorance—and there is also a fierce respect for what Wald calls "medical and religious rituals"[58] in our efforts toward healing.

The Christian faith community has a religious ritual for this kind of repair work. We call it *prayer*. When confronted with messy community and dangerous communicability, faith communities fervently resort to prayer as one of those life habits (to echo the words of Dorothy Bass) that preserves and restores hope. Nina Pham—the first nurse who contracted the Ebola virus from Thomas Duncan—is profiled on the Internet as being very religious. Her family belongs to a Catholic parish in Fort Worth, and during her illness they claimed hope through the power of prayer. When Thomas Duncan died, his family said he is now in the hands of God. In St. Louis and beyond, religious folk prayed for "justice for Michael Brown."

What is prayer, in light of the human impulse to repair?

John Shelby Spong draws a distinction between "praying" and "saying prayers" in his book *Honest Prayer*.[59] In the book, the revered theologian admits that he struggles with prayer: he is "drawn" by its power, and yet "repelled" by its forms.[60] Along with a host of other theologians and mystics, Spong reminds us that prayer is not what one *says*—prayer is what one *does*. If prayer is traditionally understood as "a human attempt to

58. Priscilla Wald, *Contagious: Cultures, Carriers, and the Outbreak Narrative* (Durham, NC: Duke University Press, 2008), 17.

59. John Shelby Spong, *Honest Prayer* (Haworth, NJ: Christianity for the Third Millennium and St. Johann Press, 2000).

60. Ibid., 15.

make contact with God,"[61] for Spong, God is not somewhere out there or up there in the nebulous skies. God is "found *in* life, not *beyond* life,"[62] and therefore prayer is most fundamentally an attempt to open oneself to the transcendent and the holy as we face into and act in this world. Theologian Douglas John Hall puts it this way: prayer is "thinking [and we might add, acting] your way into God's world."[63] The late religious educator Maria Harris put it in curricular terms: *prayer* is "a characteristic set of forms for addressing the mystery of God"; prayer fosters "*our way of being in the world before God*,"[64] a spirituality of deep communion with God and the world. And in this deep attunement, we do what liturgical theologian Marjorie Procter-Smith insists upon: we pray with our "eyes wide open" to the "patterns of domination," to "resist in order to transform, to recreate the church as communal, sociable, healthy."[65]

The clergy and faith-based activists of St. Louis nailed this when they picked up the mantra attributed to Rabbi Abraham Heschel: "Praying with our feet."

The Bible is replete with stories of people praying with their feet. Religious educator Thomas Groome lifts up one familiar tale: the parable of a persistent widow (Luke 18:1-8).[66] In this story, the exemplar of faith is a powerless widow who is annoyingly incessant in her demands for justice, so much that the judge—who is said to have no fear or respect for God or any other—finally has to give in. *The New Interpreter's Study Bible* points out a closer translation that shows the outrageous nature of this widow's persistence: "I will grant her justice," says the judge, "so that she may not finally come and slap me in the face" (18:6). Refusing to accept what un-

61. Ibid., 29.

62. Ibid. Italics in original text.

63. Douglas John Hall, *When You Pray: Thinking Your Way into God's World* (Valley Forge, PA: Judson Press, 1987).

64. Maria Harris, *Fashion Me a People: Curriculum in the Church* (Louisville, KY: Westminster/John Knox Press, 1989), 94, 103.

65. Marjorie Procter-Smith, *Praying with Our Eyes Open: Engendering Feminist Liturgical Prayer* (Nashville: Abingdon Press, 1995), 14.

66. Groome, *Will There Be Faith?*, 1.

just systems dictate as her fate, relentless in the pursuit of a corrective response, she is the example of what it means to pray, a reminder that prayer is an active pursuit of reparation, a model of how tenacious faith is a verb and not a noun. Concluding the parable, Jesus ruminates, at the end of the day, at the end of time, will there be faith like this on earth (18:8)?

A Community's Redemptive Difference: Making Good on Failed Promises

If the prayer of Jesus is illuminating for our understanding of community and communicability, then Jesus's parable of the persistent widow adds to our musings on redeemability. An evocative work of theologian David Kelsey is helpful here. In *Imagining Redemption*, Kelsey frames the question that Christians may ask when standing in the thick of what Spelman describes as ruins: "What earthly difference can Jesus make here?"[67] Expounding on foundational theological understandings of redemption, Kelsey suggests that redemption is God's work of "[making up] for the world's bad performances"; it is God's work of relieving, bailing, extracting, freeing "persons and situations from oppressive powers that bind and distort them"; it is God's fulfillment of promises made to humankind, when the world fails to deliver.[68]

The persistent widow—and, one could say, Jesus himself—illustrates for us a tenacious faith in the reparability and redeemability of unjust situations and systems. Following Kelsey's redemptive formula, Christian faith communities who want to live into their redemptive capacity might consider how they are "making up" for the world's bad performances and "making good" on the promises of new life. Better yet, we should first ask some hard questions of the church and its redeemability: What would it take to recalibrate the bad performances of communities of faith? What would it take to free communities of faith from the bondage of repressive, oppressive values, visions, and volitions? What would it take to make good

67. David H. Kelsey, *Imagining Redemption* (Louisville, KY: Westminster John Knox Press, 2005), 6.

68. Ibid., 17–19.

on the faith community's failed promise—the promise of participating with God in repairing the world?[69] In short, how do we as a church deal with our own violence and instead become redemptive communities?

Two vignettes from my theological reflectors reveal what we all recognize to be the persistent failure of Christian faith communities to live up to their redemptive potential.

Barry C.

It is no secret that the LGBT community is often marginalized or ostracized by Christian churches who hold the view that such "lifestyles" are considered contrary to the teaching of the Bible. In fact, the idea of an LGBT Christian is often considered an oxymoron. However, more and more LGBT people are reclaiming their Christian faith and embracing a more liberal view of biblical interpretation that is highly contextualized. The United Church of Christ's ONA (Open and Affirming) movement has engaged many churches in the denomination in educational and perspective widening activities and conversations to ensure that the churches are prepared to not only offer radical hospitality to the LGBT community but also help the LGBT community heal from the effects of being forced to leave their communities of faith. Additionally, there have been a large number of LGBT clergy educated in UCC seminaries to help further heal the disparities in church leadership. It is the ONA process that attracted me to this denomination and to complete my own seminary studies.

Mila R.

Since I work with marginalized populations, particularly those experiencing homelessness in St. Louis, I have noticed that churches act out "bad performances" of faith through the myths that they

69. Mary Elizabeth Moore, *Teaching as a Sacramental Act* (Cleveland: Pilgrim Press, 2004), 199–200. In Mary Elizabeth Moore's hermeneutics of sacramental teaching, the educational practices of reconstruction and repair follow God's "prophetic redemption"—"God's pull on a broken world toward wholeness—toward New Creation."

believe about marginalized populations of people. Instead of working from theologies that begin with all being created in the image of God (Imago Dei, which I am aware is not everyone's theological stance about humanity), they work with what I like to term "bootstrap theology." Bootstrap theology is a "bad performance" of faith where Christians (and others) assume all people have the ability to "pull themselves out of poverty, lack of support for mental health concerns, classist and racist ideologies, discrimination, etc." without addressing the socio-economic [among other] concerns about the human condition. Christians in America who say, "well, I have pulled myself out of (insert whatever -ism here) so others can do that as well," forget that they once counted as the "least of these," the "other" have failed to recognize the interdependence of people, both those who experience the incredible abundance of the world and those for whom scarcity is a way of life. Instead, independence, a recognition that each person has the free will to make something of themselves (and should do so without any help from others) has become the backbone of "bootstrap theology," thus opening up a world where interdependence is a choice, rather than a prerequisite of the human condition.

For evidence of hopeful endeavors, I posed the following question to the group of theological reflectors:

How/Where have you seen individuals or communities attempt to raise collective consciousness concerning the fact that the church has a moral and spiritual obligation to "make good on failed promises"?

Bruce J.

For me the immediate group/community that comes to mind is the Black Lives Matter community. The Black Lives Matter community protest, block streets, chant, and generally make their presence known to conscientize the fact that racism still exists. However, their work also involved meeting with political and local leaders.

Even in the face of others shooting down their voices in many ways, they persist in making sure people are talking and that change happens to address structural and personal racism. I can still remember the first day when folks blocked streets in Ferguson. It was a prayer service at the police department, and as the prayers were happening some young adults were getting more and more frustrated. From what I could pick up, they were getting frustrated that nothing was being done besides prayer. They were done with prayer and were ready to make real changes because one of their own, Mike Brown, was killed by police, thus the rise of protests and the Black Lives Matter movement expanding to St. Louis.

Helen C.

For several Sundays, I spent time with one of the Sunday school classes in the church: a group of octogenarians who have gathered for nearly half . . . their lives in the same room, on the same furniture, having much the same conversations. I was there to help them find a new curriculum for their group, but we found ourselves constantly talking about "young people." They were fascinated by the social conscience of a younger generation, disheartened that these young people wouldn't join their congregation, and curious and scared of them at the same time. Finally, one of the men practically shouted, "What does [large, growing area church] have that we don't have?"

"They have people who are willing to talk to their friends and strangers about their faith."

The room went silent.

The same man who had posed the question responded quietly, "We don't know how to do that."

The failure of this once-thriving church to move its people beyond community toward communicability settled upon us all.

"I know," I said. "Nobody taught you how to do that. I'm sure you've been told it's your fault for a long time. But it's not your fault. You didn't know."

> Their class as [a] whole recently participated in a teaching series I did entitled "What's Your Story?" which focused on practicing testimony, faith-sharing, and prayer through the storytelling medium. They recognize their inhibitions and fear of sharing their faith and are beginning to name it aloud. They are beginning to understand that the immanent death of their church is the result of a failed promise that churches have to spiritually develop its people, whether it's comfortable or not. (HINT: it's never comfortable.) But rather than respond with bitterness [or] exhaust themselves in scrambling to try to achieve that level of faith development, they are beginning to name their shortcoming instead and to forgive it—of the church and of themselves. And they are offering to pass on the legacy and assets of the congregation to myself and new leadership in order to begin a new congregation.
>
> In this case, it has taken generations to make good on the failed promises of the church to be a space that has a moral and spiritual obligation in communicability, not just insider community. But I believe that even the hope and promise of future conscientizing actually has the effect of forgiveness and redemption in the here and now, even for people who will not fully participate in what comes next.

As the vignettes show, repair work has past, present, and future tenses. It takes time, and it has fits and stops. At times, the vision of its *telos* appears dim for the faith community. And yet, when bolstered by the synergistic power of a collective, individuals may learn to persist toward resurrectional consciousness and insurrectional witness. When challenged by biblical and contemporary examples, faithful Christians are reminded that they are called to make redemptive difference in this world.

A question arises for the tasks of Christian religious education: How do we teach more deliberately toward this redemptive, communicable faith?

This question leads us to the focus of the next chapter: the possibilities of *educability*.

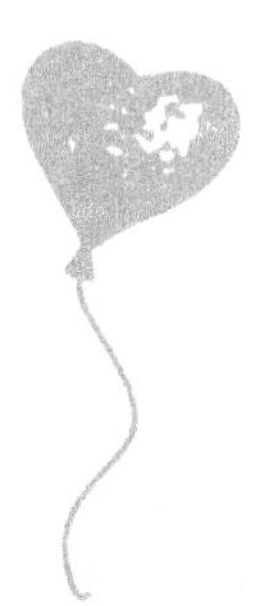

Chapter 6 Practicing Educability

Educators who refuse to transform the ugliness of human misery, social injustices, and inequalities, invariably become educators for domestication who, as Sartre so poignantly suggested, "will change nothing and will serve no one, but will succeed only in finding moral comfort in malaise."[1]

The question driving this latter part of the book has been, *What new and renewed practices of faith yield potential for the unlearning and unmaking of violence?* In the previous two chapters, we have imagined what communicable and redeemable capacities might regenerate a kind of *protested faith* for Christian communities—a faith that is tested and testing, protested and protesting in the midst of contemporary social dis-ease, a conjuncture made toxic by violence's *dis*imagination. This chapter asks how we educate toward such communicable, redeemable faith.

To do so, I propose that we think not in terms of an educational program or agenda, but of educational *curriculum* literally as "a course to be run."[2] Let us imagine what life habits and what practical wisdom in persons and communities of faith might fashion a disposition for *educability*,

1. Jean-Paul Sartre, introduction to *The Colonizers and the Colonized*, by Albert Memmi (Boston: Beacon Press, 1965), xxiv–xxv, cited in Donaldo Macedo, in his foreword to Paulo Freire, *Pedagogy of Freedom: Ethics, Democracy, and Civic Courage*, trans. Patrick Clarke, Critical Perspectives Series (Lanham, MD: Rowman & Littlefield Publishers, 1998), xxxii.

2. Maria Harris famously appropriated it, "the entire course of the church's life." *Fashion Me a People: Curriculum in the Church* (Louisville, KY: Westminster/John Knox Press, 1989), 55, 63.

what Paulo Freire calls a "critical attitude"[3] that can mobilize active participation in resurrectional, insurrectional hope. Such an approach shifts the focus away from rigid content (what we must learn) toward attunement to a "lifelong and lifewide"[4] trajectory of learning. After all, some of the most radical social reformers (Septima Clark,[5] Ella Baker, Myles Horton, Paul Robeson, Nelson Mandela, Martin Luther King Jr.) were ones who "share[d] a commitment to leading through learning."[6]

With Freire's critical attitude as our focal point, we query the dispositions or logics that condition and organize our daily habits, instincts, intuitions, and attitudes about teaching and learning. In the language of social theorist Pierre Bourdieu, we ask how our *practice* is configured and regulated by a socially structured *habitus.*[7] In so doing, we ponder the possibility of the church as an organic microcosm of faith that engenders a "special habitus"[8] of resurrection and insurrection, one that organizes and animates communicable, redeemable practices of faith.

Radical Learning and Mimetic Ecstasy

For this exploration, I propose two themes for *educability*—radical learning and mimetic ecstasy—and press for how they are evident in localized innovations.

---

3. Paulo Freire, *Education for Critical Consciousness* (London: Bloomsbury Academic, 2013), 45. Freire cites the thought of Karl Jaspers.

4. Gabriel Moran, *Living Nonviolently: Language for Resisting Violence* (Lanham, MD: Lexington Books, 2011), 167.

5. Septima Clark was an organizer of the Citizenship schools during the civil rights movement.

6. Stephen Brookfield and John D. Holst, *Radicalizing Learning: Adult Education for a Just World*, The Jossey-Bass Higher and Adult Education Series (San Francisco, CA: John Wiley, 2011), 15.

7. Pierre Bourdieu, *The Logic of Practice* (Stanford: Stanford University Press, 1990). For example, as discussed in chapter 2, the logics of colonization, enslavement, and orientalism are part and parcel of a *habitus* that choreograph the daily practices of White supremacy in the United States.

8. Pierre Bourdieu, *Pascalian Meditations* (Stanford: Stanford University Press, 2000), cited in Bowen Paulle, *Toxic Schools: High-Poverty Education in New York and Amsterdam*, Fieldwork Encounters and Discoveries (Chicago: University of Chicago Press, 2013), 189.

Radical Learning

It was a Native American story about what happens when humankind is willing to work together for the common good. A Sunday school teacher was telling it in her best melodramatic voice to a group of eager children on a Sunday morning during "children's time" in worship. As the story goes, in the beginning the Creator traversed the earth to distribute languages among different groups of inhabitants. To this one final place, the Creator decided to gift all of his (the Creator was gendered male) remaining languages, thereby creating a wonderful mix of languages and cultures. As with all good stories, there arose a problem: One day, the people of this linguistically plural place noticed with great alarm that the sky was coming down dangerously low upon them. The sky was falling, the people were scared, but they couldn't communicate with each other to avert apocalyptic disaster because they were all speaking different languages. What a multicultural dilemma.

"They didn't know what to do!"

The teacher paused for dramatic effect.

Without skipping a beat, a boy's crisp, high-pitched voice rang out from within the crowd of children: "Why don't they ask the Creator?!"

What a smart idea. But alas, that wasn't how the story was supposed to go. The teacher quickly said, "Oh, well, the Creator was resting, you see . . ."

The Creator was resting, so you can't bother him, you have to come up with a plan on your own. The child got quiet, but you know his mind was not still.

The teacher continued: thankfully, there was one smart individual within this multilingual region, who came up with a special word that everyone would say together, so that upon utterance of the word, all would understand the signal and put their shoulders together to push the sky back up to the heavens where it belonged.

The plan proceeded in this way toward its climatic end. The people of earth were saved because they had learned to work together.

The adults in that place of worship smiled with satisfaction, obviously content with the moral of the story. Human beings could do great things, they mused, if only we would work together. They signaled nods of approval of a wonderful story well told.

Just as the teacher was about to dismiss the children, the boy with the crisp, high-pitched voice shot his hand up into the air and demanded, "Well, what happened to the Creator? Where did *he* go?"

Taken by surprise, the teacher did what any average theologian probably would have done when confronted by six-year-olds who have inexhaustible supplies of questions. She stammered, "Oh, well, hmm, well, the Creator is all around us, you see. We just don't see him, that's all. Okay, boys and girls, let's go to Sunday school!"

Let's stop asking questions; let's go to Sunday school.

On most days we would laugh off this harmless exchange between an inquisitive child and his time-bound teacher, as did most of us adults in the sanctuary on that Sunday morning. Except, upon more serious reflection, it isn't very funny. Though that transaction between a lesson-driven teacher and her curiosity-starved learner appeared rather benign, it was a symptom of what Paulo Freire had diagnosed—the banality of "narration sickness," a mode of instruction in which the teacher speaks, the learners listen, the teacher "fill[s] the students with the contents of his [sic] narration"; "the student records, memorizes, and repeats" information that has been mechanically banked into their knowledge repository.[9] It is a narration sickness that chokes an "epistemological curiosity"[10] that "convokes the imagination, the emotions, and the capacity to conjecture."[11] It results in either a "magic consciousness," which "simply apprehends facts and attributes to them a superior power by which it is controlled and to which it must therefore submit,"[12] or a "naïve consciousness," an illusion of our control over a fact-based reality.[13] Absent from either of the two mind-worlds is a critical attitude, or critical consciousness, which propels self-

9. Paulo Freire, *Pedagogy of the Oppressed*, trans. Myra Bergman Ramos, new rev. 20th-anniversary ed. (New York: Continuum, 1997), 52–54.

10. Freire, *Pedagogy of Freedom*, 35.

11. Ibid., 82.

12. Freire, *Education for Critical Consciousness*, 44.

13. Ibid., 44.

reflective, self-critical dialogue—"intercommunication"—that integrates knowledge with the learner's lived reality.[14] Also deprived is the capacity to problem-pose, to query the conditions that limit one's ability to participate actively and freely in the world.[15] It might be an exaggeration, but what we had witnessed in that children's moment on that Sunday morning was a six-year-old theologian in the making, a critical mind attempting to pursue that age-old theodicy question of why a presumably powerful Creator would be absent during an earthly calamity. But in that moment, an adult told him there was no time for problem-posing in the church—not during worship, and possibly not even in Sunday school.

The narration sickness that plagues the Christian church is part of the deep structural flaws discussed in chapter 3. It is produced by the same *dis*-imagination machine that, as we saw in chapter 2, obstructs the development of critical consciousness in public education. Under this pedagogy of domestication, we witness what some educators call a "resegregation" of public schools based on racialized and gendered class division, a form of "apartheid schooling," where statistical achievement gaps dictate a market-driven corporate model of "teaching-to-the-test mania" unsupportable by substandard resources.[16] It renders toxic[17] the habitats in which young people live and learn—environments like Normandy High School, another school in an impoverished district, the status of which was downgraded to unaccredited in January 2013. It is the high school from which young Michael Brown graduated eight days before his death in August 2014.

Against the violent toxicity of *dis*imagination, we have the creative possibilities of *radical learning*. Advanced by Stephen Brookfield and

14. Ibid., 45.

15. Freire, *Pedagogy of the Oppressed*, 60, 80.

16. Peter McLaren, "The Future of the Past: Reflections on the Present State of Empire and Pedagogy," in *Critical Pedagogy: Where Are We Now?*, ed. Peter McLaren and Joe L. Kincheloe, Counterpoints: Studies in the Postmodern Theory of Education (New York: Peter Lang, 2007), 299. See also Nancy Schniedewind and Mara Sapon-Shevin, eds., *Educational Courage: Resisting the Ambush of Public Education* (Boston: Beacon Press, 2012).

17. As educational research has shown, the toxicity of educational environments systematically disadvantaged such as Normandy High can be literal, not just figurative: "chronically distressing in-school experiences . . . are negatively impacting the immune systems, neurological development, and overall well-being of students." Paulle, *Toxic Schools*, 200.

Stephen Holst, the notion of teaching toward radicalized learning is galvanized by a commitment "to create a democratic, cooperative, socialist society."[18] The commitment is socialist (and specifically anti-capitalist) in that it questions the cultural operations and economic policies that restrict learning in ways that reinforce undemocratic, inequitable social realities. Teaching that is radicalized is teaching that supports structures and practices that advance "a truly democratic future" for a just and equitable society.[19] In such democratic future, "freedom" is not just a matter of "choos[ing] to be poor or rich . . . sick or healthy . . . to vote or not to vote. . . . Rather, it is the freedom to change the very grid in which those choices are lodged."[20]

Radical learning has the following principles:

1) It engages in systemic analysis of oppressive powers and structures.
2) It commits to "democratic socialist" (anticapitalist) values.
3) It is grounded in local struggles.
4) It synthesizes theory and practice, action, and reflection.
5) It utilizes cocreative, collaborative teaching/learning modalities and materials.
6) It employs any and all methods of teaching that are appropriate to the situation and context.[21]

Stories from the local clergy elucidate these so-called radical features.

First, teaching and learning that is radical is driven by a deep-seated desire to expose power and hegemony as expressed in particular struggles (principles #1–3 above). The way to do so is not one of top-down, direc-

18. Brookfield and Holst, *Radicalizing Learning*, 107.

19. Ibid., 109.

20. McLaren, "The Future of the Past," 303.

21. Brookfield and Holst, *Radicalizing Learning*, 118–27.

tive, authoritarian exertion of power and know-how.[22] Rather, it is to get close to the immediate concerns and struggles of the people, and to facilitate multiple pathways for critical inquiry, so that insights and strategies arise inductively from the bottom up. As Pastor Helen C. witnessed, the willingness to get closer to a site of struggle for firsthand exposure often proves revelatory.

Helen C.

Our mission team, which has typically gone for weeklong service-oriented trips during the summer (think disaster clean-up and distribution centers), opted to stay [local] this year to learn about our own community through a program called Urban Forum at the nonprofit Kingdom House [which hosts many educational programs for faith and nonfaith groups from around the country]. There, they participated in service during the morning and advocacy education in the afternoon, where they wrestled with concepts of advocacy, relational discipleship, and privilege. The experience resulted in deep sharing and reflection during the evening hours . . . the type of thing a pastor dreams about: what is privilege, multiplicity of narratives, where the gospel fits into all of this. When the week was over, we all felt that the conversation had just begun, so we decided to get together to plan a worship service to share our experiences with the wider congregation. In these conversations, this team began to name, in their own words, what their call to discipleship, advocacy, and social justice was. During the worship service itself, our seventy-something-year-old lay leader named her white privilege, in her own words, before the congregation. I was stunned. In the week in which we mourn the death of Alton Sterling, Philando Castille, and five police officers murdered in Dallas, the people of the congregation were finding their voice and their sacred ground to be hope-bearers in a broken world. They were moving past helplessness and into the uncertain waters of faith. . . .

---

22. Stephen Brookfield and Stephen Preskill, *Learning as a Way of Leading: Lessons from the Struggle for Social Justice*, Jossey-Bass Higher and Adult Education Series (San Francisco: Jossey-Bass, 2009), 2–3.

> As a pastor, I must admit that it has been incredible to watch this breaking open. We are a church of retirees in deep decline, with the possibility of closure looming heavy over the congregation. But as we have let go of our own fear of the death of this particular congregation, I have seen the Spirit pour in to make us available to the larger community of the world. Our congregation is navigating and writing its own *radicalized curricula* as it lets go of old notions of what it means to be "church" or even "Christian" and embraces the gift that comes from no longer fearing death and being freed to greater purpose in the world.

Exposure alone does not lead to an emergence of critical consciousness of which Freire spoke. Experience without reflection leads to a fetishized "focalist"[23] perspective that is bereft of deeper analysis and insight. But as Pastor Helen C. witnessed, action, coupled with reflection, reinforced by *leitourgia*, made possible a buoyancy in the "uncertain waters of faith."

Such instances of radical learning unleash a collective imagination: "We must make freedom irresistible in a world where resistance to freedom is encouraged in the form of fear and the promise of security and comfort."[24] If imagination is the capacity to "give credence to alternative realities,"[25] then with reinvigorated imagination, communities learn to expose (and to confess) the toxicity of malaise and apathy that sustain the "hegemony of realism"—the mind-set that "things will never change."[26] They also expose the deceptive feel-goodness of repressive tolerance, which falsely assumes that a general attitude of tolerance is enough to dismantle the repressive power of the status quo.[27] We scrutinize the impasses that

23. Freire, *Education for Critical Consciousness*, 94.

24. Eric J. Weiner, "Critical Pedagogy and the Crisis of Imagination," in *Critical Pedagogy: Where Are We Now?*, ed. Peter McLaren and Joe L. Kincheloe, Counterpoints: Studies in the Postmodern Theory of Education (New York: Peter Lang, 2007), 65.

25. Ibid., 73–74. Weiner cites the work of Maxine Greene, *Releasing the Imagination: Essays on Education, the Arts, and Social Change*, The Jossey-Bass Education Series (San Francisco: Jossey-Bass Publishers, 1995).

26. Ibid., 69.

27. Brookfield and Holst, *Radicalizing Learning*, 191.

impede the dismantling of institutions that privilege some over others, and in doing so, like Stacey A. we may discover that what begins as critical inquiry can suddenly turn into a spiritual practice (principle #4).

Stacey A.

For the last two years, the mostly white congregation I served as a student pastor has held a weekly vigil in support of the Black Lives Matter movement. What began as a response to local police brutality after the death of Mike Brown slowly became a *spiritual practice* for a small group within the congregation to understand how white privilege affects lives and impacts systems; they gathered each week for the vigil and then shared snacks and coffee at a local business to reflect on reactions the public had to the vigil and on their own feelings. Soon, the group grew as people who saw or heard about the vigil came to participate, standing out on street corners each Saturday to hold signs that claimed the end to their silence about racism and the violence done to black bodies. This past year, the group decided to form their own local community action group to address systemic racism. They have joined in collaboration with another faith-based organization to end the school-to-prison pipeline by asking schools to stop out-of-school suspensions for younger children and asking police departments to begin implicit bias training. I have been amazed at their determination as a small group to pray (the vigil), eat together in reflection, and then love through their actions. It is sacred, it is radical, and it has become regenerative for them and for the larger community.

Finally, as already illustrated in the vignettes above, the modes and means for radical learning are "artistic, inventive," and even "speculative," thus breaking from established paradigms (principles #4–5).[28] A typical urban mission trip could become an opportunity for youth to investigate more deeply the structures of urban poverty, and to learn about the distinction between "charity" and "social justice."

28. Weiner, "Critical Pedagogy and the Crisis of Imagination," 75–76.

Barry C.

In my home church, we [have a program to host] youth groups . . . from across the country. [They] stay in our urban church [and] work in various charity and social justice agencies and participate in an educational event sponsored by the church itself. Over the past two years, I was given the opportunity to participate as co-facilitator. This year the educational event was updated with multimedia and hands-on activities to engage the topics of charity, social justice, and homelessness. With Micah 6:8 offering a biblical and theological starting point, the youth and their youth leaders are encouraged to look for examples of opportunities for charity, where social justice is needed, and where the homeless are targeted. The youth leave the event with homework, that of living into the spirit of Micah 6:8, and are challenged to consider how they can do their part to change the world for the better.

And if radical learning means negotiable, co-creative curriculum, the mediums for which can be "traditional" or "experimental," so long as it is context-appropriate, then even modest experiments can be regenerative (principle #5).[29]

Matt B.

Radicalized curricula popped up within the church that I serve, or should I say, the "church within the church" that I serve? In my 325+ person urban congregation, I observed as a group of young adults (YA) formed a social mixer group. They'd meet, bi-monthly, once to talk about a book they were reading together (often about social justice) or for a hike followed by a meal and drinks, and once to worship together. Observing the group, I noticed that, over time, the space they created encouraged vulnerability, honesty, and tenderness (no small feat for Unitarian Universalists!). Over time

29. "*Hope is an experiment* with God, with oneself, and with history. . . . An experiment tests out an object in order to bring it into the realm of experience." Jürgen Moltmann, *The Experiment Hope* (Philadelphia: Fortress Press, 1975), 187–88.

> they began to see themselves as more than just a YA group; they saw themselves as harbingers of God's love, which evolved into a covenant they share: "God's Love is a Gift & a Duty." The modest group of five to ten slowly grew to fifteen to twenty. Then they began reaching out to "YA" groups at area churches. Now, nearly fifty strong, the group regularly attends retreats together, engages in social activism, and lives out its duty to the holy gift of God's love by shaping conversation about worship and justice within the walls of its respective churches, the communities in which its members live, and the world we all share.

In sum, radical learning requires Christian faith communities to ponder what is religious and what is educational about the work that draws them together and propels them as disciple-citizens in the world.[30] Communities seeking to hone communicable, redeemable life habits for resurrectional, insurrectional hope are called to "face into the world"[31] as repairing agents, who recognize that the radical curriculum they must run is a course made for utopian social dreaming. For educators who dare to resist the implements of *dis*imagination, "hope is a choice. . . . [It] is an antidote to cynicism and despair; it is the capacity to notice or invent alternatives, and then to do something, to get busy in projects of repair."[32] To employ Elizabeth Spelman's repair words, they are propelled by the dream of educating toward *renewal* of moral conscience, *restoration* of communal agency, *reconstruction* of critical analysis, *resilience* in self-reflective dialogue, and *reconciliation* through passionate action. They are called to make conditions possible for six-year-olds to query the absence of the Creator when crisis befalls the earth—and be taken seriously by an

30. "The *church that educates for discipleship must also educate for citizenship.*" John A. Coleman, "The Two Pedagogies: Discipleship and Citizenship," in *Education for Citizenship and Discipleship*, ed. Mary C. Boys (New York: Pilgrim Press, 1989), 57. Italics in original.

31. Jack L. Seymour, *Mapping Christian Education: Approaches to Congregational Learning* (Nashville: Abingdon Press, 1997), 118.

32. Bill Ayers, "Another World Is Possible/Another Education Is Necessary," in *Educational Courage: Resisting the Ambush of Public Education*, ed. Nancy Schniedewind and Mara Sapon-Shevin (Boston: Beacon Press, 2012), 194.

adult—and for sixty-year-olds to wonder when and how they last wrestled with the question of theodicy in their own lives.

Mimetic Ecstasy

Radical learning and teaching requires a kind of reformation—a reconditioning, reprogramming, reorientation, resetting of *habitus,* such that our educational practices are no longer held captive by the logics of banking teaching, but rather are set free through resurrectional, insurrectional consciousness. As narrated in the opening of this book, there were glimpses of the instincts of this "specific habitus"[33] on the streets of Ferguson, when the faith-led Moral Monday protesters turned their bodies into mnemonic devices so that the public would not forget the suffering of Black lives.[34] The occasion was a mimetic opportunity, in that bodies were coached into what educators would call a kind of positive mimicry of protesting gestures, as several hundred people enacted a liturgy of remembrance and repentance to re-sacralize a violent living space. These practices, these instincts, seemed to have been choreographed by what I call a *mimetic ecstasy* that raises faith to the level of insurrectional witness.

Two streams of theoretical development inform this construction of mimetic ecstasy: Philip Wexler's argument for re-sacralization of culture and education, and René Girard's theory of mimesis. Wexler argues for a movement toward social re-enchantment. Drawing on the sociology of Max Weber, Wexler describes the educator as that intellectual who embodies and mediates the charisma required to raise social imagination from the ordinary to the extraordinary state. If ecstasy is the state of being pulled outside of oneself,[35] to transcend the doldrums of anesthetized existence,

33. Following Bourdieu, *specific habitus* can be understood as dispositions resulting from professional formation, situational immersion, and life experiences beyond initial, primary habitus (in the home). Paulle, *Toxic Schools,* 189.

34. Jim Wallis recounted his own experience of this event in his latest book, *America's Original Sin: Racism, White Privilege, and the Bridge to a New America* (Grand Rapids: Brazos Press, 2016), 69–72.

35. "'Ecstasy' means 'standing outside of oneself—without ceasing to be oneself—with all the elements which are united in the personal center." Paul Tillich, *Dynamics of Faith,* Harper Torchbooks (New York: Harper & Row, 1957), 7.

then it takes no less than "magic"—"a direct manipulation of forces"—to awaken us from "a world disenchanted and losing magical significance."[36] A disenchanted world is no longer capable of being "grasped by the holy"; it loses heart—courage—over the finiteness of human existence.[37] Wexler contends that religion still possesses such revolutionary magic, despite its frequent misleads.[38] Translating that claim to the level of everyday faith and faithful praxis,[39] we can assert that a society hypnotized by the *dis*-imagination machine needs ecstatic re-enchantment, powered by faith-filled life habits that allow us to re-sacralize—to make sacred again—the banality and profanity of everyday life.[40]

The magical power to elevate us to such ecstatic state can be found in what is called "good mimesis." For René Girard, whose work generated an expansive body of scholarship on mimesis, human violence is traceable to the human capacity to imitate. A working explanation of this capacity for mimetic violence or imitating violence is as follows:

> Human mimetic capacity is . . . the power to imitate what other conspecifics desire; to model our desires upon theirs; but then also—since we now so vividly represent and desire the same objects as they do—to enter into rivalry and hence also conflict with these Others. Mimetic desire is always potentially acquisitive and rivalrous—always caught in a tissue of social relationships and reciprocities.[41]

There has been robust development of Girard's original framework, including in establishing frameworks for peace-making and reconciliation.

36. Philip Wexler, "Religion as Socio-Educational Critique: A Weberian Example," in *Critical Pedagogy: Where Are We Now?*, ed. Peter McLaren and Joe L. Kincheloe, Counterpoints: Studies in the Postmodern Theory of Education (New York: Peter Lang, 2007), 51–52.

37. Tillich, *Dynamics of Faith*, 17, 20–21, 58.

38. Philip Wexler, *Holy Sparks: Social Theory, Education, and Religion* (New York: St. Martin's Press, 1996), 14.

39. *Praxis* is used here to echo the Freirean synthesis of reflection and action.

40. Wexler, *Holy Sparks: Social Theory, Education, and Religion*, 6.

41. Pierpaolo Antonello and Paul Gifford, *How We Became Human: Mimetic Theory and the Science of Evolutionary Origins, capitalization:* "Studies in Violence, Mimesis, and Culture" (East Lansing: Michigan State University Press, 2015), ProQuest ebrary, accessed June 10, 2016.

An account of such work in the context of Northern Ireland by Derick Wilson is relevant here: "'Good mimesis' has the dual task of modeling concretely new models of freedom between different identities, thus meeting the intellectual and theological challenges of promoting the ways of 'communion' and cutting out the old ways of 'crucifixion.'"[42] Good mimesis is nurtured by a "contrast-culture"—

> which is relational and centered on trust—a culture of relationships where people experience a freedom and openness with different Others; where there are experiences of learning together in often very robust relationships; so many fragile embryos capable of growing into new relationships and structures, re-linking very divided people and the traditions they come from.[43]

Such a symbiotic ecosystem is an enriching soil for members to model themselves on toward freedom, rather than mimic one another into violent destruction.

To avert the assumption that mimetic learning is devoid of originality and self-determinism, I draw on Homi Bhabha's notion of mimicry in colonial situations. Colonial mimicry is the mode by which a colonial system imposes a representation of itself upon the colonized other; yet it is an ambivalent "camouflage" representation that is "almost the same, but not quite."[44] Ironically, this dismissiveness of the other's so-called less-than mimesis (Black/Brown semblance of White presence[45]) results in a partial recognition of the colonizer's authoritarian presence, an opportunity for subversiveness when a colonized subject mimics or mimes the

---

42. R. Kaptein, with D. Morrow, *On the Way of Freedom* (Dublin: Columba Press, 1993), 119–24, cited in Derick Wilson, "Communities of Contrast: Modeling Reconciliation in Northern Ireland," in *How We Became Human*, ed. Pierpaolo Antonello and Paul Gifford (East Lansing: Michigan State University Press, 2015).

43. Kaptein, *On the Way of Freedom*, 116.

44. Homi K. Bhabha, *The Location of Culture* (New York: Routledge, 1994), 122. In the end, the system of partial mimesis leaves the Bible an implement of European colonial representation, one that is enforced upon colonized subjects, yet one also manipulated in the appropriation of the colonized. "Still everyone would gladly receive a Bible. And why? – that he [sic] may lay it up as a curiosity for a few pice; or use it for waste paper." Bhabha, *The Location of Culture*, 131, citing a missionary report from Bengal, *The Missionary Register*, May 1817, 186.

45. Bhabha, *The Location of Culture*, 129.

identity, culture, or meaning-making systems of their colonizer.[46] To use the language of pedagogic condition, whether it is coerced or willing, the embrace of colonial *habitus* is never an exact imitation.

Whereas Bhabha attends to mimetic tensions between colonizer and colonized, I focus on the possibility of originality in mimicry. That is to say, there is always room for creative improvisation when we attempt to imitate another's meaning-making actions. No act can hold proprietary control over emulating actions. Leaders can never command exact imitation from followers, just as teachers cannot demand obtuse parroting from learners. Instead, mimetic learning is an act of "fractal mirroring"—no pattern of repetition is ever the same, yet each act encourages another. After all, *catechesis* is derived from the Greek *katecheo*, "meaning to teach by 'echoing' a tradition."[47]

Altogether, positive mimesis (with room for creative fractal mirroring) and ecstatic re-enchantment yield the possibility of *mimetic ecstasy*—the capacity for persons in nurturing communities to look at each other and model themselves after the freeing actions that awaken all to the vitality and sacredness of their life together. After all, as protest movements prove, no one acts alone. It takes the linking of arms, the kinetic energy shared between bodies pressed tightly against one another in shared responsibility,[48] the calling out of suffering through the language of grief and anger, the invocation to ancestors of suffering and hope, the petitions to the Spirit of a living God. Standing in the thick of such forms of carnal *leitourgia*, an individual may find herself in mystic, cosmic union with

46. "The ambivalence of mimicry—almost but not quite—suggests that the fetishized colonial culture is potentially and strategically an insurgent counter-appeal. What I have called its 'identity-effects' are always crucially *split*. Under cover of camouflage, mimicry, like the fetish, is a part- object that radically revalues the normative knowledges of the priority of race, writing, history. For the fetish mimes the forms of authority at the point at which it deauthorizes them. Similarly, mimicry rearticulates presence in terms of its 'otherness', that which it disavows." Ibid., 129–30.

47. Thomas H. Groome, *Will There Be Faith? A New Vision for Educating and Growing Disciples* (New York, NY: HarperOne, an imprint of HarperCollins, 2011), 102–3.

48. In Cantonese, *koinonia* is translated as *tuen kai*, a combination of "solidarity" and "responsibility." David Ng, "A Path of Concentric Circles: Toward an Autobiographical Theology of Community," in *Journeys at the Margin: Toward an Autobiographical Theology in American-Asian Perspective*, ed. Peter C. Phan and Jung Young Lee (Collegeville: Liturgical Press, 1999), 102.

the arc of the universe, which people of faith believe always bends toward justice and restoration.

For glimpses of such mimetic ecstasy, I asked the group of theological reflectors, *How/Where have you witnessed instances of positive mimicry, in which individuals or groups feel motivated, inspired, empowered to do something because they "saw someone else do it"?*

The examples they offered ranged from irresistible joy witnessed during protest, to cautious actions—inspired by leading examples—that lead churches to "more than what they bargained for."

Yvonne K.

August 10, 2015, was one day after the murder of unarmed black youth Michael Brown by armed white officer Darren Wilson, and a Moral Monday demonstration at a major courthouse in St. Louis. Prominent clergy who supported the Ferguson uprising were there to march and be arrested in civil disobedience, to urge the Department of Justice to "do your job" and prosecute Darren Wilson. Clergy modelled resistance, leading the march with local activists and children, clambering over barricades, and conducting a sit-in at the courthouse. Clergy and activists motivated the public with chants, inspired them by lending theological significance to the action, and empowered them with a ritual where everyone anointed each other with holy oil before climbing over the barricade. The barricade was a series of metal fences, chained to each other, separating the public from the courthouse guarded by police, a literal representation of police blocking the people from justice. Osagyefo Sekou and Cornel West led the way by hurdling over the barrier, with Rev. Maria [pseudonym] and the public following suit. Sekou and Maria realized that the police were not moving to arrest them and they began to dance and frolic on the sidewalk, their joy infecting the public, impishly daring them to join. And join, the community did, climbing over the barricade, clapping and chanting freely, before linking arms for the sit-in, claiming and surrounding the courthouse on all sides. The positive mimicry was indeed a happy contagion, with several people who were not intending to cross the barrier deciding to cross the barrier anyway. One person was a bystander to the march until he decided to join in, crossing the barrier, and getting arrested with the seasoned protestors and trained clergy too. We often speak about fighting for justice, but what we sometimes forget is that glimpses of liberation can spark so much joy that *participation is irresistible.*

Or consider Mila R.'s witness on positive mimicry.

Mila R.

"Positive mimicry" is the embodiment of the church I serve. It is a congregation that takes a curriculum of "eat, pray, love" seriously, but also struggles to create new ideas in which those values can be embodied, so positive mimicry offers them a way to engage the world. Perhaps the best example of this "follow the leader" style of mission has happened with feeding those experiencing homelessness in St. Louis. Though the congregation would say that it's "my" (Mila's) baby, so to speak, it's because they see how excited, saddened, and passionate I am about engaging the issues surrounding homelessness that they are also inspired to do the same. For instance, we are doing a month of providing sixty meals weekly for [an outreach center] on Sundays. At first, I thought the response would be small, a few people packing bags and then lugging them to my vehicle to be passed out later that evening. The first day got a response of fifteen people, one who later traveled with me to hand out the bags . . . that same night. The next week the youth group and at least seven other adults responded by preparing the bags of food, two of whom served the meals with me that night. And even though we only need sixty meals, somehow I can't stop them at that number. The first week we made seventy-eight meals and the next sixty-four; I have said to myself many times that this abundance is the power of the Spirit. "Positive mimicry" functions as a way for churches to "safely explore" the gospel and for the Spirit to do her work of providing "more than the church bargained for" in passionate action and embodied love.

Occupying Religious Education: Local Innovations

Radical learning, good mimesis, and mimetic ecstasy characterize a faith community conditioned by a *habitus* that is open to resurrectional, insurrectional possibility. Whether it be imitating holy foolishness during protest, or being infected with the happy contagion of service through small acts, radical learning through positive mimesis yields potential for ecstatic re-enchantment. Considering some of the recent portraits of the contemporary religious landscape (as briefly surveyed in chapter 3), one wonders whether churches that fret over declining membership and dwindling educational programs have focused so much on niche-marketing the gospel that they have lost the imagination and capacity for research and development. The analogy came to me in a conversation with a chemist, whose job in his company's R&D department is to experiment, innovate, and make what could be described as serial mistakes until a solution emerges that meets a particular need. The R&D department doesn't worry about whether products will sell, he said. That's the business of marketing. In the language of radical learning, R&D is dedicated to artistic, inventive, speculative exploration.

Perhaps it is in this renewed commitment to intentional research and development—experimentation and risk-taking in the service of innovation—that communities of faith will find opportunities to re-habituate themselves to radical learning, to good mimesis, to ecstatic re-enchantment. Perhaps churches might take some cues from the improvisational nature of recent protest movements—from the Occupy movement to Black Lives Matter. The reasons for which these movements were critiqued may be the very attributes that enhance the church's capacity to be locally innovative.

For one, protest movements understand themselves to be communities *in transit.* Activists are constantly on the move, locating themselves wherever there is struggle. The church as a learning community[49] could take after the transient nature of street movements, or, for that matter, of

49. An expression made familiar by religious educator Norma Cook Everist and her book, *The Church as Learning Community: A Comprehensive Guide to Christian Education* (Nashville: Abingdon Press, 2002).

lives displaced by either voluntary or coerced migration. Members of such *ekklesia*

> understand themselves as travelers, shuttling back and forth, in and out of in-between spaces, tending and attending to the concerns of one another's real lives. Occupying such spaces invites a spirituality of *intentional dislocation*—purposeful movement from the comforts of fixed foundations, establishment, endowment, and permanence—for co-existence in a world enlived by fluid, shifting, multivalent, multifarious stories of faith and culture. Intentional dislocation assumes a practice of border-crossing that dislodges us from our comfort zones, interrupting complacency with the status quo. Intentional dislocation grows an understanding of church that is always in transit.[50]

At the same time, even with the embrace of transience, action is always localized within specific times and places. It is organically improvisational, yet the improv is performed out of well-honed *habitus*. It is responsive to specific situations, contexts, and needs—an "organic hybridity"[51] that characterizes the subtle negotiations and contestations of words (ideas and commitments) within plural and polarizing worlds.[52] Christian faith communities can become "enabling communities of practice"[53] when they are willing to harness resources toward such localized improvisations. Christopher Baker describes this as a faith community acting out of its "local performative theology": its engagement is "locally rooted," but "the

50. HyeRan Kim-Cragg and Mai-Anh Le Tran, "Turning to the Other," in *Complex Identities in a Shifting World: Practical Theological Perspectives*, ed. Robert Mager, Pamela Couture, Pamela McCarroll, and Natalie Wigg-Stevenson (Zurich: Lit Verlag GmbH & Co. KG Wien, 2015), 136.

51. M. M. Bakhtin and Michael Holquist, *The Dialogic Imagination: Four Essays*, trans. Caryl Emerson and Michael Holquist, University of Texas Press Slavic Series (Austin: University of Texas Press, 1981), 360.

52. See my discussion of "organic hybridity" for contemporary Christian religious education in Mai-Anh Le Tran, "Narrating Lives, Narrating Faith: 'Organic Hybridity' for Contemporary Christian Religious Education," *Religious Education* 105, no. 2 (2010). Paulo Freire also famously stated that to read the *word* enables us to read the *world*. See Paulo Freire, *Teachers as Cultural Workers: Letters to Those Who Dare Teach*, trans. Donaldo Macedo, Dale Koike, and Alexandre Oliveira, The Edge, Critical Studies in Educational Theory (Boulder: Westview, 1998), 18.

53. Tran, "Narrating Lives, Narrating Faith," 191.

knowledge and experience acquired locally is part of an analysis that will transform the locality at a political, economic, social and spiritual level."[54]

Mick E.

While on the recent All-In Tour I had the opportunity to visit an organization in Greensboro, North Carolina, called Faith Action International House. Faith Action serves and accompanies thousands of our newest immigrant neighbors, while educating and connecting their diverse community across lines of culture and faith—turning strangers into neighbors. One aspect of [Faith Action's task] is working with congregations to become Stranger to Neighbor Congregations that engage in education, dialogue, and intercultural exchange with immigrants to become welcoming to the immigrants in their community as well as advocates taking action with their immigrant neighbors. Another aspect of their work that is perhaps more relevant to the question is an ID program they created. Recognizing that undocumented people live in fear of discovery, imprisonment, and deportation, they created IDs for undocumented people to carry as a means for them to no longer be fearful, and to begin feeling at home in their community. They then worked with local law enforcement and the local government to have these IDs be a valid form of identification. They succeeded and now hold ID drives in cooperation with local law enforcement through which thousands of immigrants in Greensboro obtain this now legal form of identification. That program then caught on in other parts of the state. The downside presently is that North Carolina's radicalized state legislature is now seeking to pass a law to nullify those IDs. The bill was brought before the state legislature the day we visited Faith Action, [and] now threatens to return members of the Greensboro community to a state of fear, uncertainty, and instability.

---

54. Christopher Richard Baker, *The Hybrid Church in the City: Third Space Thinking* (Aldershot/Burlington: Ashgate, 2007), 126.

Localized engagement, however, must also be globally networked. That is another lesson from the educative work of movements. With the advancement of globalization, technology, social media, and international travel, there has emerged a new sociospatial pattern of "heterolocalism," in which "ethnic or religious communities can maintain close ties without spatial propinquity, scattered instead over large urban, national, or international domains."[55] It is why Palestinian activists came to express solidarity with the Black Lives Matter actions in St. Louis. It is the concept behind such formational programs as the Youth Hope-Builders Academy of the Interdenominational Theological Center in Atlanta that incorporates the element of "raising global consciousness and building Pan-African awareness and relationships"—what they call "kin-to-kin connections"—in their comprehensive programs for the empowerment of African American youth.[56] It is what motivates a predominantly White UCC congregation in Webster Groves, Missouri, to connect with the resources of the Samuel DeWitt Proctor Conference[57] in order to gain local and national insight into the establishment of a new Freedom School for St. Louis. It is also what inspired small acts like that of Yuna R., a young pastor in Japan, who organized her community to fold one thousand cranes to express grief and hope in the wake of Michael Brown's shooting death.[58]

Finally, a recurrent rallying cry of protest is #ShutItDown—a demand to shut down institutions, policies, and processes that no longer serve the needs of the people. Quite different from the logic of "success, expediency, performance, [and] profit"[59] of the market economy, which

55. Charles Lloyd Cohen, *Gods in America: Religious Pluralism in the United States* (New York: Oxford University Press, 2013), 86.

56. Youth Hope Builders Academy, accessed August 17, 2016, http://youthshopebuildersacademy.blogspot.com/.

57. Samuel DeWitt Proctor Conference, accessed February 2, 2017, http://sdpconference.info/.

58. For a spirited argument for the emergence of locally innovative "progressive" faith communities, see Hal Taussig, *A New Spiritual Home: Progressive Christianity at the Grass Roots* (Santa Rosa, CA: Polebridge Press, 2006). To make his point about the vitality of the progressive Christian movement, Taussig catalogs one thousand such communities that exist across the country.

59. R. S. Sugirtharajah, *Postcolonial Configurations: An Alternative Way of Reading the Bible and Doing Theology* (London: SCM Press, 2003), 32.

quite readily endorses closures based on assessment of yields and returns, #ShutItDown declares defunct establishments that no longer serve the "99 percent"—or, perhaps closer to the biblical mandate, the *bottom* 1 percent, "the least of these." If education for discipleship becomes more about filling church pews with dues-paying members, or about growing internally similar affinity groups that thrive on a gospel-lite version of activism-lite, rather than about messy, gritty, gutsy faith-driven participation in the world, then such church education has lost sight of the prophetic mandate by which Jesus fashioned his own life of discipleship: bringing good news to the poor, releasing the captives, healing infirmities, letting the oppressed go free, proclaiming God's Jubilee.[60]

In a way, #ShutItDown is a contemporary cry for Jubilee. For Catholic religious educator Maria Harris, the heart of Jubilee teachings is spiritual, political, and economic attunement to the forces of one's time and place. Her mantra captures this understanding: "The demand is *liberation*; the emphasis is *connectedness*; the corrective is *suffering*; the power is *imagination*; and the vocation is *tikkun olam*—the repair of the world."[61] Given the signs of our times, Harris's description of the demand, emphasis, corrective, power, and vocation of Jubilee remains relevant as ever. For example, protest movements reveal the restless demands of the multitude for liberation from social, economic, political, and environmental violence. Widespread communicable dis-ease exposes the underlying septic condition of apathy, *apatheia*—the state of being physically, psychically, and ethically "unaffected by external influences,"[62] an indifference to connection. The "omnipresence of pain and suffering"[63] serves as a reality check against naïve hope or uncritical optimism. Suffering serves as a corrective lens in that manner: it is *not* a precondition for liberation, but a pervasive reality that tests our capacity to be moved by *pathos*. As Harris frames it,

60. Luke 4:18-19.

61. Maria Harris, *Proclaim Jubilee!: A Spirituality for the Twenty-First Century* (Louisville, KY: Westminster John Knox Press, 1996), 4.

62. Moltmann, *The Experiment Hope*, 73.

63. Harris, *Proclaim Jubilee!: A Spirituality for the Twenty-First Century*, 10.

confronting human suffering forces us to slow down; it ushers us into fear and dread; it has the potential to fuel our passion to say "Stop!" to the madness of injustice and violence.[64]

Mobilized by pathos—the opposite of apathy—artistic imagination undergirds our active response. Imagination is not fantasy-filled or voyeuristic look-sees into others' pain. Rather, it is "a set of bodily actions" that give flesh to visions and dreams of freedom, granting and receiving forgiveness, mercy and justice, and jubilation.[65] The vocation—the ultimate goal—of the above movements of educational praxis is the restoration of the world, *tikkun olam*. The Jewish mystic Isaac Luria imagines the repairing of the world as the task of "picking up the [shattered and scattered] shards of creation and trying to mend and transform the vessels by refashioning them."[66]

Pastor Yuna R.'s story of local innovation speaks to Jubilee's demand for our attunement to God's re-creating work in the land—and the land (dust/dirt/soil) that is our bodies:

> I have witnessed that local innovations of ideas take on generative power in a farm. The farm is based on permanent agriculture that follows a natural ecosystem. Vegetables are neither fed chemical fertilizer nor natural manure. The farmers encourage them to grow by themselves and believe their own original potential to grow. In a market, a uniform size of crop production is required. They should have almost the same size, weight, and colors. But the crop productions made from the permanent agriculture are so different. When I worked in the permanent agriculture farm, I could (had to) use my own hands to cultivate lands, plant seeds, and harvest the crops. While working, I thought about all of my worries and didn't talk a lot. It is like meditation. It is like having a conversation and dialogue with God through the nature that was made by God. How beautiful and strong God's creation in this world on earth! This slow, calm, and strict farming effects a change in our life gradually. When we touch God's creation directly, we may be closer to God. God touches our heart through the farming and helps us to change and renew our mind.

64. Ibid., 10–11.

65. Ibid., 14.

66. Ibid., 15.

Pastor Bruce J. writes of regenerative work that has starts and stops:

> I have seen, and am still seeing, local innovations for some parts of the Ferguson community through a colleague of mine. Right after Michael Brown was killed and the uprising started, this colleague felt the call to start a weekly meal, conversation, and study around folks' experiences around race relations. Each week he would gather with whoever showed up, from the church he was serving and elsewhere, share a potluck meal (with some food provided), and talk if folks needed to talk (about police in general, about economic disparity, about their own emotions and hurts, etc.). If it seemed like a good time to do some learning, they would watch documentaries about [the history of racism] in the country and locally. The model was of course not new necessarily, but it was transforming to where some of the "regulars" are now planting a church and forming a "work ministry" where they go around Ferguson, see who needs some work done, and do it. There were starts and stops, the weekly meal is on pause, but regenerative work was and is being done.

Jürgen Moltmann reminds us that "if someone wants to be a Christian, don't send [them] into the churches, but into the slums. . . . That is where [they] will find Christ."[67] Since its early founding movements, the Christian church has continued to look in every direction for clues on how to locate regenerative hope in the midst of debilitating suffering and decline. From whence does our creative force come when the sky is falling down upon us? For the band of petrified Galileans desperate for a re-enchantment of their world, a problem-posing moment came in the form of a question: "Why are you standing there, looking toward heaven?" (Acts 1:11). Perhaps the ecstasy they had hoped to mimic was a literal transcendence from this-worldly anxieties. Perhaps they had forgotten the radicalized curriculum of a teacher who was constantly in-transit, a teacher who ignited resurrectional, insurrectional power from within the multitude, a teacher who exhorted them to go bear witness to the utopian social dream that is God's kin(g)dom being realized on this earth.

The early followers of Jesus—and those who've come after them—exhibit their best capacities for educability when they actively echoed

67. Moltmann, *The Experiment Hope*, 2.

through good mimesis that tradition of communicable, redeemable witness-bearing, instead of distorting it into a world-dominating gospel. They had been instructed to proclaim through daily life habits a message superbly encapsulated later by Freire: "The world is not finished. It is always in the process of becoming."[68] The *habitus*, the internal meaning structure, that choreographs such mimetic ecstasy is not an idolatry of activism, an over-confidence in our human ability to "solve all problems through right programs and actions."[69] Nor is it sentimental "coddling" that eases the demands of hard struggle.[70] Rather, theirs, and ours now, is a *habitus* of "responsible *hope*"[71] in many possible futures, of faith hinged upon critical memory of the past, of *love* enfleshed through painstaking, day-to-day, shard-by-shard repair work. Conditioned by this *habitus* of faith, hope, and love, religious educators recall the words of Paulo Freire:

> One of the most important tasks of critical educational practice is to make possible the conditions in which the learners . . . engage in the experience of assuming themselves as social, historical, thinking, communicating, transformative, creative persons; dreamers of possible utopias, capable of being angry because of a capacity to love.[72]

To love and to fight, they are the virtues of *courage*, "the daring self-affirmation of one's [and the other's] own being in spite of the powers of 'nonbeing.'"[73]

68. Freire, *Pedagogy of Freedom*, 72.
69. Moltmann, *The Experiment Hope*, 70.
70. Freire, *Teachers as Cultural Workers*, 15.
71. Moltmann, *The Experiment Hope*, 187.
72. Freire, *Pedagogy of Freedom*, 45.
73. Freire, *Teachers as Cultural Workers*, 41; Tillich, *Dynamics of Faith*, 17.

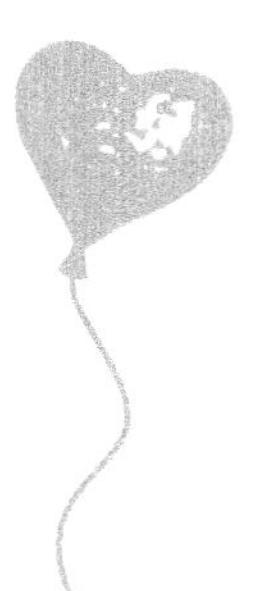

Conclusion "World Turned Upside Down"

Every religious educator aspires to educate toward transformation—after all, who would want to teach toward stasis? Yet transformation is both promising and threatening. In our zeal to transform, we forget that some ruins are irreparable and irredeemable, as Spelman points out.[1] Moreover, what is to distinguish the power of renewing transformation from power of destructive change?

In *The Christian Imagination*, theologian Willie James Jennings writes of the Andean notion of *pachacuti*—which means "world turned around" or "world turned upside down."[2] *Pachacuti* was the native Andean's term to refer to the epoch-turning arrival of the Spanish, who brought to the New World "Old World pathogens": "smallpox, influenza, tuberculosis, measles, and other diseases."[3] It is a familiar story of cultures collapsing and imaginations fossilizing under colonial contact. When lives are extinguished in ominous physical and social death,[4] we wonder how resurrection is possible. However, with tenacious faith, we follow Jennings's

1. Elizabeth V. Spelman, *Repair: The Impulse to Restore in a Fragile World* (Boston: Beacon Press, 2002), 102.

2. Willie James Jennings, *The Christian Imagination: Theology and the Origins of Race* (New Haven, CT: Yale University Press, 2010), ebook edition, chap. 2.

3. Ibid., ebook edition, chap. 2.

4. For the *Washington Post*'s tracking of fatal shootings by police officers: www.washingtonpost.com/graphics/national/police-shootings-2016/.

imagination and look back to the origin of that idyllic community that ate, prayed, and loved in Acts 2: an origin located in an explosive, uncontainable in-breaking of the Spirit. Jennings's words are persuasive:

> If a world caught in the unrelenting exchange system of violence was to be overcome, then here was the very means God would use to overcome violence—by the introduction of a new reality of belonging that drew together different peoples into a way of life that intercepted ancient bonds and redrew them around the body of Jesus and in the power of the Spirit.[5]

Here, Jennings draws us to the redemptive power of the Spirit, which reconfigures community around a new space of intimate knowledge and intimate relationships, the center of which is the body of Jesus—a body resurrected and "vindicated"[6] against repressive powers, a body that proclaimed the rule of God on this earth in the here-and-now. In this new redemptive space, the human calculus of who is significant, who is made in the image of God, who is pathogen or contagion, is turned upside down. In this space, the redemptive communicability of the Spirit reconfigures fragile human community. In this redemptive space, we may discover that *faith* is the state of being "grasped by the holy," in which our ultimate concern is the essential aliveness of self and neighbor—whom we are to love, not as much as we love ourselves, but *as though they were our very selves.*[7] In bearing witness to resurrectional, insurrectional power, made paradigmatic in the proclamation that Jesus is a "Resurrected One," we set our hearts on a critical hope that from the ruins of death, God restores life.[8]

A story outside of the Christian faith tradition, linking the local and the global, illumines a heart set against the violence of *dis*imagination. It's

5. Jennings, *The Christian Imagination*, ebook edition, chap. 6.

6. Jack L. Seymour, *Teaching the Way of Jesus: Educating Christians for Faithful Living* (Nashville: Abingdon Press, 2014), 157.

7. See Nicholas Wolterstorff's treatment of this notion of agapist love in *Justice in Love,* Emory University Studies in Law and Religion (Grand Rapids: William B. Eerdmans, 2011).

8. See Seymour's encapsulation of the paradigmatic proclamation of Jesus in *Teaching the Way of Jesus: Educating Christians for Faithful Living* (Nashville: Abingdon Press, 2014), 150–58.

a story of a life in transit, of bodily witness, of critical hope, redemptive faith, and a yearning for communicable love.

Bolinao 52

Between 1975 and 1995, over a million Vietnamese attempted to leave their country by boat in the aftermath of tumultuous regime change.[9] Nearly half of those who left never made it to land. In 1988, Ms. Tùng Trinh and a band of 110 Vietnamese compatriots pushed out to sea. After thirty-seven days at sea, their boat ran out of gas and food supplies. On day 19, they drifted past the naval vessel USS *Dubuque*, which was on its way to join Operation Free Will in the Persian Gulf, under the command of Captain Alex Balian. Allegedly due to miscommunications, the captain did not allow the drifting refugees to embark, but instead left them with food rations and directions for the nearest landmark. By the time the boat reached the shores of Bolinao in the Philippines, only fifty-two of the original 110 persons remained, and word spread quickly that they had resorted to cannibalism. Minh, a male leader who took over control of the boat and orchestrated a regimen of water bailing and rationing of human flesh, was held in isolation in the Philippines, was denied entry into the United States, and subsequently resettled in Europe. Captain Balian was court-martialed by the US Navy for dereliction of duty and was found guilty and relieved of command. Yet the "Bolinao 52" survivors signed a petition for the captain to be pardoned.

The documentary *Bolinao 52* by Vietnamese American filmmaker Duc Huu Nguyen recounts the group's journey through terror.[10] Ms. Tùng Trinh, one of the protagonists featured in the film, is one of very few individuals willing to give words to the experience. After all, some things are unsayable, some experiences unstoryable. "We were dying one by one," Ms. Tùng recalled in the film. She beseeched every transcendent being known to her: *"Cau xin Phat Troi, cau xin Chua, cau xin Duc Me...cau xin ca hu hon cua ban dong hanh, giup do cho con thuyen"—Buddha, God*

9. 2015 marked the fortieth anniversary of what many diasporic Vietnamese refer to as the "fall of Saigon," or the official end of the war on April 30, 1975.

10. *Bolinao 52,* directed by Duc Huu Nguyen (RHIMP Productions, 2010).

of Heaven, Mary Mother of God, and the spirits of all those who had already died, please help this boat. "I could only pray for a miracle . . . ," she said, as rations of human urine and human flesh kept most of them only barely conscious.

"Did it taste good?!" people would ask Ms. Tùng. The violence of trauma is repeated in a different register by socially enforced pressures to remember and recount. After all, anamnesis can be traumatic. She had no choice, she insisted: to keep her alive, her brother would slap her in the face to bring her back to consciousness, and would then quickly shove a piece of flesh into her mouth and force her to swallow. Ms. Tùng's meal was a literal consumption of violent death, ironically, for the sake of remaining alive. However, what she and the other survivors of Bolinao 52 consumed was not just human flesh, but what Christians might call the *sins* perpetuated by all of humanity at that time—the violation of life through cycles of war, of military and colonial occupation, of biochemical weaponry, of ecological plundering, of geopolitical manipulations, of social callousness, of one captain's rule-bound disregard for desperate fellow seafarers and the routinized execution of his orders—all together, of moral *dis*imagination. The absorption of humanity's violence into these marked bodies is largely lost to the consciousness of the global community, perhaps also to religious communities, and even to those of us who waged principled protest against war. We were transfixed by the public pedagogies offered by Coppola's commercialized *Apocalypse Now*, distracted by benevolent humanitarianism, or succumbed to compassion fatigue.

In 2005, Ms. Tùng Trinh returned to Bolinao to thank the Filipino fisher folk who had rescued her and the others. "When you eat a piece of fruit, remember who planted the tree," she cited the familiar Vietnamese adage. She also wanted to "*cúng*" her deceased compatriots—a ritual of spirit veneration practiced in Vietnam's folk religion, choreographed by offerings of food, incense, and prayers to/for the ghostly spirits of the deceased—so that their wandering souls might find peaceful rest. Not too many people know or care about the fate of these lost spirits.

Small Acts

Ms. Tùng did what some religious educators believe we are in the business of doing, or what we think we are teaching others to do. Against the inertia of social *dis*imagination, she risked what practical theologians have called "mighty stories, dangerous rituals."[11] That is, she dared to tell stories and enact rituals as a way to remember and reestablish her right to freedom, dignity, and integrity, those fundamental human rights violated by the traumas of terror.

First, like religious educators, Ms. Tùng mustered up courage to tell stories, but her stories are about flesh consumed by violence, and her storytelling defies certitude about right and wrong. On her boat, there were saviors and cannibals. The cultural apparatuses of the *dis*imagination machine tell her that she and companions on that fateful boat were worth *less*. On any given day, a first-rate, first-world naval implement of military power and political duty out-values drifting asylum-seekers sardined in a fishing boat. And yet, tipping the scale of significance, Ms. Tùng shares her story to remain human in the eyes of others. She is not flesh-consuming vermin or vulture; do not render her inhumane, or *un*human. Christians recognize this fierce insistence: the human being is an image of God—*imago Dei*—the only imaging of the Divine that is permissible.[12] A violation of that image is a violation of God. Now, while Christians may rely on the Spirit as Paraclete to assist them in the remembrance, narration, and participation in the Eucharistic meal as a way to transform the trauma of violence into eschatological hope,[13] Ms. Tùng calls upon the spirits of her deceased companions, those with whom she literally and figuratively "broke flesh." In doing so, she teaches us about the struggle to remember against the forces of *dis*imagination. Perhaps in similar ways, the spirits of those like Michael Brown will teach religious educators by becoming

11. Herbert Anderson and Edward Foley, *Mighty Stories, Dangerous Rituals: Weaving Together the Human and the Divine* (San Francisco: Jossey-Bass, 1998).

12. John A. Coleman, "The Two Pedagogies: Discipleship and Citizenship," in *Education for Citizenship and Discipleship*, ed. Mary C. Boys (New York: Pilgrim Press, 1989), 56.

13. Andrea Bieler, "Remembering Violence: Practical Theological Considerations," in *After Violence: Religion, Trauma and Reconciliation*, ed. Andrea Bieler, Christian Bingel, and Hans-Martin Gutmann (Leipzig: Evangelische Verlagsanstalt, 2011), 56–58.

haunting mnemonic devices that jolt our passive surrender to mentacide, the organized erasure of historical memory, an abetting of ignorance and apathy that legitimizes our reduction of the other to something less than worthless.

Second, also like religious educators, Ms. Tùng facilitated culturo-religious rituals. As a syncretistic Buddhist-and-spirit-venerating worshipper who appeals to Christian deities, she is haunted by ghostly spirits of departed friends, and improvises rituals to restore the sacred intimacies shared with companions on that terrifying journey. Rituals are dangerous when they disrupt the banality of everyday religious and cultural habits. Ms. Tùng's altar to "*cúng*" or venerate the deceased is akin to the roadside memorials that pop up spontaneously, improvisationally at sites of death. Not so much as props for thana-voyeurism, these altars and memorials challenge passive observers of violence to participate actively in small gestures of defiance against it. Ms. Tùng's ritualistic improvisation reminds religious educators that the faith gestures we teach can be either signs of anesthetized religious imagination, or liturgies of protest against this- and other-worldly principalities.

Third, just as religious educators assist persons in accessing sources and resources for daily moral-ethical decision-making, Ms. Tùng attempted to recalibrate her ethical compass for new life in new worlds by seeking out the Filipino fishing villagers who rescued her and the American sailors on the USS *Dubuque* who bypassed her. Unlike many other heroic survivors of violence who somehow find conciliatory or compensatory resolution to their tragic stories, Ms. Tùng speaks of the past with moral ambivalence. The quiet *han*[14] of having been bypassed and forgotten by humanity does not quite dissipate. And yet, in her self-storying, one does not find cynicism, nihilism, or delusional hope. Instead, Ms. Tùng shows willingness to take up what Jewish philosopher Peter Ochs calls "small actions," or attempts to "act in the fashion of human beings . . . who did not lose their

14. *Han* is a concept that emerged out of Korean liberationist *minjung* theology. It refers to the anguish of a "wounded heart," a "frustrated hope," defined as follows by theologian Andrew Sung Park: "Han is the division of the tissue of the heart caused by abuse, exploitation, and violence. It is the wound to feelings and self-dignity." *The Wounded Heart of God: The Asian Concept of Han and the Christian Doctrine of Sin* (Nashville: Abingdon Press, 1993), 19.

integrity *as* human beings" in the face of violence.[15] They are ordinary acts in extraordinary times—"saying no here, protesting there, enduring here, organizing there"—but they are actions "guided by a norm or an ethic" that has not succumbed to "the demoralizing weight of terror."[16] They are the small acts that yield power—and Gabriel Moran reminds us that power means possibility[17]—small acts that bolster possibility for resurrectional hope.

Taking a cue from this one woman's small actions, religious educators should turn to the task of problematizing our pedagogical complicity in *dis*imagination. Christian religious educators might want to call into question routinized educational infrastructures (Foster's catechetical cultures) that preserve normative status quo, that initiate members into practices of violence in the service of group identity, interest, or ideology.[18] We might want to scrutinize the explicit, implicit, or null curricula that organize people's forgetting, that breed fear through *mis*education, that conveniently erase our faith tradition's complicity in violence. We might expose how particular religious rituals trivialize, justify, normalize, routinize, or sanctify violence. We might ask whether religious education is anesthetizing moral agency, such that we are only good at drawing on the mores of religious traditions to denounce violence rhetorically, yet do very little about conditioned "habits of mind" buttressed by "tacit assumptions and expectations" that sustain static, exclusive, undifferentiating, impermeable points of view about the world.[19]

15. Peter Ochs, "Small Acts against Terror: Jewish Reflections on a Christian Witness," in *Surviving Terror: Hope and Justice in a World of Violence*, ed. Victoria Lee Erickson and Michelle Lim Jones (Grand Rapids: Brazos Press, 2002), 290–91.

16. Ibid., 291.

17. Gabriel Moran, *Living Nonviolently: Language for Resisting Violence* (Lanham, MD: Lexington Books, 2011), 49.

18. Cf. Hannah Arendt, *On Violence* (New York: Harcourt, 1970), 67; Jack David Eller, *Cruel Creeds, Virtuous Violence: Religious Violence across Culture and History* (Amherst: Prometheus Books, 2010).

19. Jack Mezirow, *Learning as Transformation: Critical Perspectives on a Theory in Progress*, The Jossey-Bass Higher and Adult Education Series (San Francisco: Jossey-Bass, 2000), 4, 17–19.

Against violence's *dis*imagination, we continue to ask, What new and renewed critical agendas for religious knowing and religious praxis do we need to educate faithful persons to set their hearts upon for earnest small acts toward resurrectional, insurrectional hope in this world?

Dream Work

Writing about another kind of socio-political haunting—the United States' "Forgotten War" in Korea—sociologist Grace M. Cho describes the hermeneutic of "dream work," or the researcher's ability to see things into being, especially to see that which has been violently suppressed within the spectacles of empirical descriptions. Through dream work, Cho caught on to folkloric descriptions of *honbul*—"ghost flames," or "flickering lights [that] rise up from the ground, usually at the site of a massacre."[20] The truth is found "somewhere between science and the supernatural," Cho writes: "In places where buried bodies are heavily concentrated, the remains have changed the chemical makeup of the earth, causing the soil to ignite. Through ghost flames, the spirits of the dead release their grief and rage, their *han*, into the world."[21]

The church's educational ministry occurs within a conjuncture in which blood- and rain-soaked streets give off ghost flames, haunting the public imagination with quiet grief and resounding rage for a more just, less violent world. Contemporary cries of those most vulnerable under repressive powers echo those found in the Christian biblical narratives: the cry of the Hebrew slaves, the sackcloth of Ritzpah, the laments of Rachel. If religious education is "the reshaping of life's forms with end and without end,"[22] "to link lives of individuals and communities to larger, ultimate realities and purposes,"[23] if it is necessarily an "intervention in

20. Grace M. Cho, *Haunting the Korean Diaspora: Shame, Secrecy, and the Forgotten War* (Minneapolis: University of Minnesota Press, 2008), 16.

21. Ibid.

22. Moran, *Living Nonviolently*, 167.

23. Sara Little, *To Set One's Heart: Belief and Teaching in the Church* (Atlanta: John Knox Press, 1983), 21.

the world," as Paulo Freire announced long ago,[24] then we need religious educators who are deeply attuned to ghostly apparitions of suppressed memories and subjugated experiences, and are committed to resurrecting deadened spirits. Against the enduring "pathological praxis of hostile passion and cruelty,"[25] embedded within what theologian Dorothee Sölle calls "structures of violence that rule this world,"[26] we need pedagogies that help us narrate the anguish, ritualize principled protest, and reinvest in what Evelyn Parker calls "emancipatory hope" in the future.[27]

Theologian Harvey Cox tells us that we live in the "age of the Spirit."[28] In this age, faith is awe, faith is wonder, faith is a conscious hope and confidence in God's in-breaking. Religions that facilitate such faith do not offer dogma; instead, they offer narratives that help people make meaning, rituals to intensify human experiences, and ethical guides for daily living. In this age of the Spirit, a faith community is redemptive when it makes good on performances and promises that the world *and* the community itself fail to deliver. In this age of the Spirit, a faith community is redemptive when it teaches people—through the curricula of eating, praying, and loving—how to set their hearts on repairing the broken shards of human situations and systems.

Against the relentless pedagogies of *dis*imagination, persons and communities of faith are called to persist in communicable love, redeemable faith, and educable hope. We make accessible and manifest[29] stories and rituals of tenacious faith, of life-wise, life-tested agency, of spiritual resilience and resistance, of a stubborn determination to dream for a future in which

24. Paulo Freire, *Pedagogy of Freedom: Ethics, Democracy, and Civic Courage*, trans. Patrick Clarke, Critical Perspectives Series (Lanham, MD: Rowman & Littlefield, 1998), 90–91.

25. Cheryl A. Kirk-Duggan, *Misbegotten Anguish: A Theology and Ethics of Violence* (St. Louis, MO: Chalice Press, 2001), 28.

26. Dorothee Sölle, *Death by Bread Alone: Texts and Reflections on Religious Experience* (Philadelphia: Fortress Press, 1978), 6.

27. Evelyn L. Parker, *Trouble Don't Last Always: Emancipatory Hope among African American Adolescents* (Cleveland: Pilgrim Press, 2003).

28. Harvey Gallagher Cox, *The Future of Faith* (New York: HarperOne, 2009).

29. Boys, *Educating in Faith*, 193.

Everyone has enough to eat
Debts are released
There is deliverance from unfair trials
Human communities repent from our violent allergies to one another
In our openness and vulnerability, we seek to be grasped
  by hallowed presence in this world.
And despite what the *dis*imagination machine may portend,
  we insist that this world belongs to a creating and creative God,
  and as such, it is full of powerful possibility and glorious splendor.

Let the people of God say "Amen."

And let Christian religious educators remind the people of what "Amen" means.

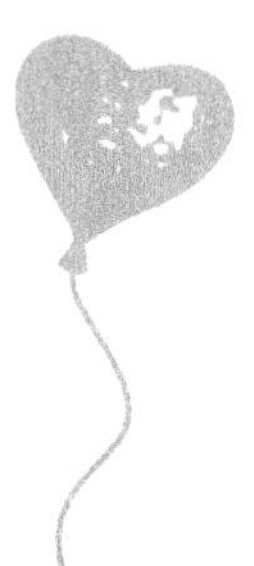

Appendix

What Does It Mean to Teach for Hearts Reset on the Promises of Gospel?

1. We call violence by its many names and expose its stealth powers. We recognize that violence to the image of God is a violation of God.
2. We confess that we live as though called to a *ministry of death* rather than a *ministry of freedom* (2 Cor 3). We confess that

    - we practice distorted love (we exercise control/domination, assert superiority);
    - we practice constricting worship (we think we have exclusive access to God and that God only heeds our rituals and sacrifices);
    - we practice closed table (we hoard, we dictate the menu and manners for eating, our dietary needs deplete the resources of others);
    - we are apathetic to how our way of life is in effect draining life sources from others; and
    - we are idolatrous: we believe that we—and only we—are the image of God.

3. We commit to a ministry of teaching and living in which

    - we practice love through risky contact with our neighbors;
    - we worship as though our livelihood depends on it—we pray with our feet, the joys and laments of the world become our prayers,

the streets are our sanctuaries, we make sacred that which violence desecrates;

- we eat in such a way that enables for all to eat;
- we form communities without borders; and
- we participate in making good on the promises of gospel.

4. We teach toward agency, not because we believe in the power of humans but because we believe in the power of being human, imaged and powered by God.
5. We teach toward capacities to imagine and to question, to ask "what happened?" and "what if?" It's through these capacities that we can
    - imagine/enact stories and counter-stories of tenacious faith and persistent courage in the face of death-dealing violence;
    - imagine/enact the power of life over death, freedom over enslavement;
    - imagine the sacredness of all lives, all times, all spaces; and
    - imagine/enact definitive *nos* to destructive powers and principalities.
6. We teach toward ecstatic love for this messy world—not for worldly love. We remember that God made it good and continues to work actively in sustaining that goodness.
7. We organize our life habits according to the ethical "dream" that
    - *everyone has enough to eat;*
    - *no one suffers from crippling debts;*
    - *there are no more unfair trials;*
    - *we make up for the ways in which we have been "allergic" to one another;*

- *we seek to be grasped by hallowed presence in this world; and*
- *we recognize that power and glory do not belong to us.*

Reflection Questions

These were reflection questions posed to the fourteen theological reflectors, who shared vignettes as a response to these themes. Consider these, and expand on them, for brave conversations within local communities. Consider how they might yield ideas for small but enduring actions toward communicable love, redeemable faith, and educable hope.

Practicing Communicability

1. How or where have you witnessed faith communities wrestle with the risks and vulnerabilities of human contact?
2. How or where have you witnessed practices of *love* that yield regenerative power in the face of contagious violence?
3. How or where have you witnessed practices of *worship* that enacts the realm of God in the here and now—worship that breaks assumptions about where God might be found, about how we might have access to God, or who has better access to God?
4. How or where have you witnessed *table practices* that dismantle barriers and bring about restoration and reconciliation?

Practicing Redeemability

1. How or where have you witnessed the faith community struggle with failed promises and/or bad performances of faith?
2. How or where have you witnessed the faith community demonstrate a *resurrectional imagination*—the capacity to see life in the face of death-dealing situations?

3. How or where have you seen the power of *insurrectional witness*—testimonies and actions that defy an oppressive status quo and insist on an alternative, life-giving reality?

Practicing Educability

1. How or where have you seen faith communities come to recognize that they have an obligation to "make good" on and "make up" for failed performances of gospel?
2. How or where have you seen evidence of *radicalized curricula*—teaching and learning that stokes moral conscience, communal agency, critical analysis, self-reflective dialogue, and passionate action toward reconciliation?
3. How or where have you witnessed *positive mimicry*—in which individuals or groups are motivated, inspired, empowered to do something because they saw someone else do it? What conditions made that possible?
4. How or where have you witnessed local innovations of *small actions* that seem risky or uncertain at first but took on generative power through slow, incremental, yet effective change? What conditions made possible the steady persistence?

CPSIA information can be obtained
at www.ICGtesting.com
Printed in the USA
LVOW03s1316210317
527871LV00003B/3/P

9 781501 832468